D0837624

THE LIVING DEAD

THE LIVING DEAD

SWITCHED OFF ZONED OUT
THE SHOCKING TRUTH ABOUT OFFICE LIFE

DAVID BOLCHOVER

CAPSTONE

Published in 2005 by Capstone Publishing Limited (a Wiley Company), The Atrium, Southern Gate, Chichester, West Sussex, PO19 8SQ, UK
Phone (+44) 1243 779777

Copyright © 2005 David Bolchover

Email (for orders and customer service enquires): cs-books@wiley.co.uk
Visit our Home Page on www.wiley.co.uk or www.wiley.com

All Rights Reserved. No part of this publication may be reproduced, stored in a retrieval system or transmitted in any form or by any means, electronic, mechanical, photocopying, recording, scanning or otherwise, except under the terms of the Copyright Licensing Agency Ltd, 90 Tottenham Court Road, London, W1P 0LP, UK, without the permission in writing of the Publisher. Requests to the Publisher should be addressed to the Permissions Department John Wiley & Sons, Ltd, The Atrium, Southern Gate, Chichester, West Sussex, PO19 8SQ, UK, or e-mailed to permreq@wiley.co.uk, or faxed to (44) 1243 770620.

Designations used by companies to distinguish their products are often claimed as trademarks. All brand names and product names used in this book are trade names, service marks, trademarks or registered trademarks of their respective owners. The Publisher is not associated with any product or vendor mentioned in this book.

This publication is designed to provide accurate and authoritative information in regard to the subject matter covered. It is sold on the understanding that the Publisher is not engaged in rendering professional services. If professional advice or other expert assistance is required, the services of a competent professional should be sought.

David Bolchover has asserted his right under the Copyright, Designs and Patents Act 1988, to be identified as the author of this work.

Other Wiley Editorial Offices
John Wiley & Sons, Inc. 111 River Street, Hoboken, NJ 07030, USA
Jossey-Bass, 989 Market Street, San Francisco, CA 94103-1741, USA
Wiley-VCH Verlag GmbH, Pappellaee 3, D-69469 Weinheim, Germany
John Wiley & Sons Australia Ltd, 42 McDougall Street, Milton, Queensland 4064, Australia
John Wiley & Sons (Asia) Pte Ltd, 2 Clementi Loop #02-01, Jin Xing Distripark, Singapore 129809
John Wiley & Sons Canada Ltd, 22 Worcester Road, Etobicoke, Ontario, Canada, M9W 1L1

Wiley also publishes its books in a variety of electronic formats. Some content that appears in print may not be available in electronic books.

Library of Congress Cataloging-in-Publication Data is available

British Library Cataloguing in Publication Data

A catalogue record for this book is available from the British Library

ISBN-13: 978-1-84112-656-2
ISBN-10: 1-84112-656-X

Typeset in Adobe Garamond Pro 12/15pt by Sparks, Oxford (www.sparks.co.uk)

This book is printed on acid-free paper responsibly manufactured from sustainable forestry in which at least two trees are planted for each one used for paper production.

MIX
Paper from
responsible sources
FSC
www.fsc.org   FSC® C013604

Lüdger Roedder
03/2015
Jersey City, NJ

To the forgotten talents of the Living Dead

CONTENTS

ACKNOWLEDGEMENTS

I would like to thank several people for helping and encouraging me to write this book. Robin Shepherd and Jo Rosenfelder provided detailed and predictably intelligent comments on each chapter. The time and effort they both devoted to this are greatly appreciated. Jim Poyser, Johnny Maginn and James Read also gave me invaluable assistance in formulating my ideas at various stages of the writing process.

Most of all, I owe a huge debt of gratitude to my wife, Janie. If it were not for her love, support and belief in me, I could well still be experiencing my very own Living Death. For this, and for so much else, I thank her from the bottom of my heart. Now that this book is completed, I look forward to spending more precious time with her and with our beautiful baby daughter, Yael.

David Bolchover writes frequently on business and management issues for *The Times* and *The Sunday Times* as well as a number of other national newspapers and specialist publications. His first book, *The 90-Minute Manager*, outlines the lessons that business managers can learn from football managers. Previously, he was employed for several years in a large office. But now he wants to do something with his life.

CHAPTER 1

UNEARTHING THE LAST TABOO

Without work, all life goes rotten. But when work is soulless, life stifles and dies.

Albert Camus

e are living in an era of workplace stress. Gone are the days when men worked in nine to five jobs, and returned to the home looked after all day by their wives. Now both partners have to juggle their work/life balance – with jobs that stretch them to the very limit, coupled with the task of looking after children and their domestic life.

The increasing competitiveness of the modern economy has rendered people slaves to their workplaces. Companies now have to exact every last drop of effort from their employees in order to survive. People are being sacrificed on the altar of profitability. Their employees acquiesce, frightened of the financial consequences, in an expensive world, if they opt out of the system. An exhausted nation is trapped in a never-ending rat race.

At least, that's what we are told in countless stories peddled by the media. And this narrative might indeed describe the reality for some, maybe even most.

But the truth for many millions is very different. They may be menial clerical workers, they may be more senior. They may be lowly-paid, they may be handsomely paid. They may be men, they may be women. They may work in the private sector, or maybe in the public sector. But what they all have in common is that they go into a large office somewhere in the world every weekday, they go to their desk at the same time, they leave at the same time. And in between, they do pretty much nothing. Zilch. The Big Zero.

Nobody knows what they do, nobody really cares. You don't hear about these people, because who wants to boast that they don't do anything at work? Their working lives are mindlessly boring, utterly pointless and without meaning, their abilities are completely wasted. Their home lives may be happy and fulfilled, but at work they are the people that time forgot. They contribute next to nothing. They are the Living Dead.

This book is dedicated to their long-forgotten talents.

The living death rate

'Millions are idle, but it's comforting to know that most of them have jobs.'

Source unknown

Before entering into any analysis of the reasons why the Living Dead are not really talked about, and before examining the causes and the repercussions of their existence, let's first of all set out just a few of the bare facts. After all, as any psychotherapist worth his salt would tell you, in order to analyze and solve a problem it is first necessary to acknowledge its very existence. And proof of the prevalence of the Living Dead is out there for all of us to see, if only we were to choose not to avert our gaze and allow ourselves instead to piece together the jigsaw of isolated statistics to form a true picture of working life for many.

Indeed, hardly a week goes by without some statistic appearing which indicates that the Living Dead constitute a sizeable community. How's about this for a start? 14.6% of US workers admit to surfing non work-related Internet sites *constantly*.[1] 70 million have Internet access at work in the US, so that would work out at the small matter of 10,220,000 people earning their salary by playing computer poker and researching their family tree. In another survey, employers report that workers spend *on average* 8.3 hours, or more than one entire workday, accessing non work-related websites each week.[2] Given that offices usually contain many people, many of which are over a certain age, and are not natural users of the Internet, this is surely a quite staggering figure. Moreover, we can surely inflate the figures even further as so many, as we shall see later, are unlikely to be wholly honest about the reality of their working lives, even for the purposes of a survey.

Let's not try, as many do, to ignore the meaning of these figures and argue that the vast majority of workplace Internet users are generally just taking a well-earned and necessary breather before they throw themselves back into their mad, busy working day. If you want a true indication of the extent of the Living Dead sub-culture, just type the three words 'bored at work' into your Google search engine. But a word of warning – only do it if you've got a typical office job and have a good couple of days to spare to wade through the plethora of 'bored at work' sites and chatrooms.

I could go on – 56.3% of US employees send up to 5 personal e-mails per day, a further 18.7% send up to 20, and 7.2% actually find time in their impossibly crowded diary to send more than 20. 35.2% of the workforce receive more than 5 personal e-mails a day. 10.3% are so enviably popular that they receive more than 20 a day.[3]

Oh, that workplace stress. No wonder everybody is dying of it. They are literally dying of boredom. The Internet and e-mail are just two of the distractions people will turn to when they have nothing or little to do. Animated conversation with colleagues, phone calls to friends, nipping out of the office for a 'few minutes', that dentist appointment (you'd think people in offices should all look like Donny Osmond, the number of times they go to the dentist), or for the more senior among us, 'a business meeting in town'.

Thinking about it, why actually even bother turning up for work at all? You have to travel in on the sweaty underground or packed train, and then when you get there, you spend all day working to avoid working, when the truth is that nobody would probably notice if you weren't there anyway. Why not just spend the day at Alton Towers? You will certainly find yourself among like-minded people, as one in three of all mid-week visitors to the theme park have also taken the day off work on a dishonest pretext. Three-quarters of the self-confessed skivers surveyed at Alton Towers told bosses they were sick, as their excuse for failing to turn up for work, with dental appointments, a family bereavement and domestic emergencies among the other popular ruses. Interestingly, only one in ten felt guilty about bunking off, with the remainder not giving it a second thought.[4]

Presumably this level of remorse is felt by a similar proportion of those in the UK who make the nine million 'suspicious' or 'questionable' requests each year for sick notes from their doctors.[5] That's nine million, approximately the population of Sweden. Let's try to visualize the sheer scale of this. Excuse me, the population of Sweden, can you all just line up in orderly fashion; men here, women here, children over there, inhabitants of Gothenburg can you come this way please, just be patient Sven Goran, hold on Bjorn, all in good time, you will all eventually be given the opportunity to ask for a note to give to your employer saying you are ill, when you are not in fact ill.

If that killjoy quack wants to act like Miss Goody Two Shoes and refuses to sign off on your 'illness', then just go home and stick some arsenic in Rover's Pedigree Chum. Over half of the UK's 14.5 million pet owners said that they would need between two and five days off work to grieve for their pet, while 10% said they would need as much as two weeks.[6] We're all stressed out, up to our eyes in work and utterly indispensable of course, but when Tiddles shuffles his way through the cat-flap of heaven, one naturally has to take just a little time out to recharge the old emotional batteries.

All this slacking, of course, only applies to certain indolent types. At least we can rely on those thrusting young professionals, burning with new ideas, creativity and ambition, and untouched by corporate cynicism. Not according to another survey we can't. A third of UK young professionals are hungover at least twice a week on working days (ever tried doing any work with a hangover?); and an additional 48% of those polled admitted to being the worse for drink at least one working day a week. Two-thirds admitted to having called in sick due to alcohol at least once in the previous month.[7]

Oh, but alcohol is so twentieth century, don't you think? A survey in *Time Out* magazine revealed that one in three people have taken drugs such as Ecstasy, cocaine, cannabis and amyl nitrate at work.[8] These are clearly not just hard-core addicts. In a study by Quest Diagnostics Inc. in the United States, a company that checks millions of workplace drug tests annually, 40% of all casual users (people who use drugs just once a month) still choose to do it at work. 19.6% of people who take drugs at work don't even have the courtesy to leave their desks when they do it. (Afterwards they might be seen getting out of their chairs and dancing around a bit, I assume).

Drugs might be used by some as an antidote to workplace boredom, but quite apart from the obvious health risks, they do have a further unwanted side-effect – they could well get in the way of a man's fundamental right to have a decent kip at his desk. One in four Europeans has fallen asleep in the workplace, according to a 2004 survey.[9] 'Long workdays, routine tasks, meetings that drag on (Jesus, tell me about it), and staring into the monitor are prompting workers around Europe to fall asleep at their workplace,' said one of the survey's co-authors, Internet jobs site *Jobline*.

The poll showed 24% of respondents had fallen asleep either at their desk, in a meeting or in the toilet. 39% said they had not fallen asleep at work (oh, come on! it's only a survey guys, nobody's going to tell) but did have to make an effort to stay awake. As for the remaining 37%, they were no doubt residing snugly in the Land of Nod when the question was asked.

Sick of being one of the Living Dead for years on end? Then why not have a bit of a change and just be Dead Dead instead? In January 2004, a Finnish tax auditor died at his desk, and it took the hundred people who worked on the same floor two days to notice,[10] during which time the corpse no doubt outperformed his much less dynamic colleagues to win Employee of the Week, and the motivational prize of a weekend of embalming at the health spa of his choice.

By the way, if you think that prostitutes are the only people who are paid to have sex, think again. According to a survey of 30,000 workers undertaken by a professor of sociology at California State University, one in five respondents had had sex with a co-worker during work hours. Full sex, that is. 44% of men and 35% of women have had at least some sexual contact at work.[11] 44%! And all the while, there was naïve little me sitting there spending my working day researching material for my book on football management, furtively reading *Bob Paisley: Manager of the Millennium* and other such towering works of literature. Bob, if you happen to be listening up there in that great big dug-out in the sky, sporting your celestial flat cap, I hope you feel a sense of moral worth in preventing me from fulfilling all my sordid sexual fantasies.

If you happen to be too physically repulsive to get the real thing, or are just boringly loyal to your partner at home, don't worry, there's always the net. According to Spysoftware.com, a PC surveillance company, 70% of Internet porn sites are accessed during the 9 to 5 working day. At the Department for (No) Work and Pensions, officials investigating the internet use of their employees discovered that 2.3 million pages of pornographic material had been accessed over eight months in 2004.[12] It pains me even to mention it, but I dread to think about levels of masturbation in the workplace. No one has bothered doing a survey on this yet, as far as I am aware. Don't worry though – in the age of openness that will doubtless come soon, I see future headlines vividly: '73% of male US workers snap one off in office toilet'; '53% of European office workers knock 'em out every day.'

The Conspiracy of Silence

'As scarce as truth is, the supply has always been in excess
of the demand.'
Josh Billings (pseudonym of Henry Wheeler Shaw),
American humorist

There seem to be no limits to what we talk about these days. Paedophilia,
incest, our own alcohol or drug problem, child abuse, you name it. All
these are issues that were previously deemed too painful or vulgar to
discuss. Now our airwaves are filled with debate about subjects that past
generations would have found impossible to stomach. Oprah Winfrey and
Jerry Springer are instantly familiar symbols of this modern phenomenon
of openness.

Yet, despite many of our own personal experiences and the ready avail-
ability of relevant statistics, the reality of the workplace seems to be the
last taboo in our society. We just seem to skirt over the fact that there are
a mass of people who go in to an office every day and suffer from dispiriting, de-energizing, mindless tedium. Isn't this worth talking about? If we
can talk about somebody's aunt having lesbian sex with their sister, surely
we can find a way to talk about this. After all, quite apart from the huge
corporate and economic effects of this large-scale inactivity, the whole
experience surely also has a destructive effect on the individual concerned.
I should know, because I've been there. To be honest, you can actually feel
pretty much as dead as it is possible to feel while you are still breathing.
Does that sound a bit over-dramatic to you? You're lucky then. You've
obviously never been a member of the Living Dead brigade. You can read
this book as an interested observer, rather than as one of the millions who
has actually been there, done nothing and got the T-shirt. You will only be
able to imagine, rather than feel, the weariness and apathy caused by the
nine-to-five nothingness, the interminable clock-watching, the incessant
time-killing, the growing cynicism and bitterness.

Although you will hear countless stories in the media about workplace
stress, about the difficulties of sustaining a healthy work/life balance in
the modern world, about the physical dangers of overwork and its negative social consequences, you will not hear discussion on underwork of a

parallel and equally serious reality. The reality of underwork, of the gross under-utilization of talent, of the criminal waste of human potential, of the slow strangling of drive, creativity and ambition.

Why *is* there such silence on this issue? The reasons are varied and complex, all resting on a fundamental dishonesty and wilful blindness that is bound up with the world of work, but is increasingly absent in the rest of our open-up-and-tell-all society.

Our first participants in this dishonesty are our Great Leaders, the people at the top of the corporate world. They have a vested interest in perpetuating the idea that their company has a dynamic, creative and motivated workforce. They are clearly not going to say otherwise to the media and to investors, for fear of damaging the 'brand'. Moreover, living in denial and embracing the myth elevates their very own self-image. My organization is dynamic and motivated. I am the head of that organization. Therefore I must be absolutely superb.

The Great Leaders have also been recently encouraged by the latest management book fad – not to concern themselves overly with the nitty-gritty of what goes on at the grass roots. The fashionable, but misguided, philosophy of 'Leadership' allows those at the top of organizations to ignore the chronic level of demotivation and sluggishness beneath them, and instead to prance around exuding authority, making 'keynote' presentations, transmitting an example, developing their 'leadership style' and acting as a symbol of the 'culture' that doesn't even exist.

Of course, our Great Leaders are encouraged in these meaningless endeavours by the worst kind of consultants and gurus who make money out of appealing to their self-importance and their sense of mission. These consultants are not stupid. The people at the top of the organization have their hands on the purse strings and will pay huge sums to have their individual marketability increased and their egos massaged. Consultants will find it difficult, on the other hand, to attract fees by highlighting large-scale and very basic structural problems with the company concerned. Telling the potential buyer of the consultancy services that their company is suffering from a widespread plague of torpor and lethargy is not the easiest way to win business. It's firstly a little insulting, and the change required to rectify the situation, if it is indeed at all curable, would be so all-encompassing and radical that it would probably scare the buyer off. Far better to stick to 'change' programmes that have the added bonus of not really changing anything. After all, the status quo still serves these consultants and our Great Leaders very well indeed.

The same could be said for the writers of business management books, our Esteemed Gurus. The motivation behind the vast majority of business books is that they can, if successful, lead to a significant promotion of the author's brand name and hence to lucrative consultancy contracts. So, for the same reason as the consultants themselves, the preferred angle of the Esteemed Guru is to offer lazy, space-filling platitudes and superficial solutions to relatively minor problems, thus shying away from any honest and fundamental appraisal of the reality of the working culture in many of our companies. Maybe he will be able to get some well-paid speaking engagements on the back of his book as well. This will give him ample opportunity to hide the vacuity of substance with a slick, confident presentation and a few impressive-sounding buzzwords.

There is also within the business book genre, and indeed within the business world in general, a strong tendency to focus, often unrealistically, on the optimistic and the positive. The plethora of self-help books promising to transform the reader's working life for the better, or of business books trotting out dull anecdotes of personal or corporate success both reflect this tendency. OK, it's good to be positive. But not, surely, at the expense of ignoring the negative, and allowing it to fester and spread.

In reality though, most consultants and Esteemed Gurus, like our Great Leaders, don't actually come into contact much with the average worker. Many of them have only a very distant memory of working at the sharp end of an organization. They are now overseeing or analyzing corporate strategy from their very comfortable ivory tower vantage point. It may be a view that is utterly detached from day-to-day reality, but being up there doesn't half pay the bills.

The media might also have played a significant role in the suppression of the truth by distorting, unintentionally, the popular perception of the modern-day workplace. The print and broadcast media operate in a genuinely competitive industry, with regularly recurring tight deadlines producing a culture of intensity and pressure. Persistent hard work is therefore a feature of many journalists' existence, and it is only natural that this experience makes them firstly, more disposed to writing or broadcasting stories about overwork, and then to exaggerating its significance in the wider world.

Also participating in the denial about the reality of the workplace are those with a political axe to grind. First, the liberal left. Capitalism, according to their world view, is inherently exploitative, squeezing the last drop of sweat out of an exhausted workforce. These commentators depict the corporate world as voraciously profit-driven, treating people as cash cows to be milked dry and then consigned to the abattoir. This perspective conveniently ignores two large chunks of the workforce. First, those people who derive energy and meaning from working hard and who value their relationship with their employer. Second, those millions of Living Dead who are lost in the cracks of cumbersome, incompetently managed, money-squandering organizations that allow them to sit around doing next to nothing for years on end. The ruthless capitalist world of the left-wing imagination simply would not tolerate such waste. And anyway, going around exposing the existence of gross inefficiency might encourage more rationalization and redundancy. So for the *lefterati* and their trade union comrades, too much contemplation or discussion of underwork is to be avoided.

Right-wing commentators are often guilty too of letting political prejudice cloud their view of reality. Their standard line is that the super-efficient, hard-nosed private sector is stretching itself to the limit to pay for those for all those meaningless but highly paid public sector sinecures, whose lucky beneficiaries spend all day doing nothing. 'The public and private sectors could hardly be more different', wrote Leo McKinstry in the *Daily Mail*. 'Private companies … live or die by success in the market place. Facing intense competition, the commercial manager will soon be out of a job if he does not bring in the customers. But the public executive has none of this pressure. Cushioned by his monopoly on local services and his largesse from the public purse, he enjoys a sense of security unknown in the business world, with little to fear from failure.' It might be difficult to argue with McKinstry's analysis of waste in the state sector, but one wonders if he would have the same romanticized notion of how the private sector works if he were to reflect honestly on a year spent in a large company office. He describes capitalism as it should be, straight from the Adam Smith textbook, but not, sadly, how it often is.

You would think that company middle managers might have a better grip on what is actually going on. But just as for the leaders and gurus, there is nothing to be gained for them in confronting or articulating the truth. On the one hand they are nominally charged with people management, and too much talk of lots of people not really doing anything will therefore reflect badly on them, and will present them with an onerous and possibly insurmountable challenge. On the other hand, the fact is that middle managers in larger companies are not usually rewarded for the performance of those under their supervision. If they are, that will not be the sole determinant of their remuneration. So why should they bother even flagging up the prevalence of inactivity? Even if they solve the problem, they wouldn't be properly compensated.

Besides, middle managers are rarely natural people managers, and usually lack a developed sense of empathy with their charges. They have been selected for promotion to 'management' because they were good at their job and were ambitious. There is no reason to assume that they will have the aptitude or willingness to manage others. That was not a consideration in their promotion.

Ambitious middle managers continue doing the work they were doing before promotion – what they enjoyed doing, what they were good at doing and earned the initial recognition. They look up, not down. There is no mileage in managing the minions, or even observing or analyzing what they are doing all day. They instinctively recognize the rules of the corporate political game. They form alliances with those above them, forming a quid pro quo, you-scratch-my-back relationship with those who can act as their Powerful Patrons and promote them further. Meanwhile, many beneath them are left to rot.

And finally there are my former comrades, the massed ranks of the Living Dead. They are not going to make a big deal of it either. It doesn't make sense for them to let their bosses know that they are effectively being paid for no reason, as such outpourings of honesty might get a load off their chest but could leave them with no job at the end of it. You could say that getting out is still the best option, but this can involve a significant risk or an initially substantial reduction in living standards which many, especially those with financial responsibilities, might understandably be unwilling to accept.

As is the case for the Great Leaders, there is also the issue of self-image for the Living Dead. Our work still forms the majority of our waking lives, and is even now the basis for how we are judged by many in society. So we are not going to admit, maybe even to ourselves, that our daily sojourn to the office is completely futile. We often scrabble around all day trying to look busy to convince our bosses and ourselves that we are useful workers. Outside the office, honesty about our working lives is not the best way to make friends and win the hearts of the opposite sex. Dynamism and energy are sexy, not drooped shoulders, yawns and the recounting of entire days spent looking through windows.

Often too, the Living Dead occupy quite senior and prestigious roles. As my own story will reveal in the next chapter, I myself was paid very well and had job titles and positions that would have sounded impressive to many when I told them what I did. Why would I have wanted to damage all that just for the sake of a little honesty? So when people delved a little more deeply into the details of my job, I rarely offered them even a glimpse of the reality.

Obviously, I talked more candidly to my very close friends and family. They would sometimes be in exactly the same boat and so I had willing and sympathetic listeners. But the discussion never left this immediate and intimate sphere, which goes a long way to explaining why there is no public discussion of the Living Dead. Doing nothing at work is something you only talk about to your nearest and dearest if at all, whereas people queue up to admit that they performed oral sex on a television celebrity, or to write books about their past as a vicious football hooligan.

All this workplace dishonesty has its very own language. It's called jargon. George Orwell once said that 'the greatest enemy of clear language is insincerity.' That is the reason why we talk clearly and normally to our family, friends and to the man in the corner shop, but we talk in a completely different way as soon as we step through the office door. I assume I am not alone in saying that I understand pretty much everything I read in the newspapers, or hear on television or the radio, or in conversation with even my most intellectual friends; but I spent most business meetings in a state of utter bafflement.

For jargon is the language of image creation and dissembling, not honesty or transparency. If we were working in a company consisting of two people, there would be no jargon. There would be no point saying, 'Going forward, we intend to revisit our "core competencies", or "we envision rolling this product out", or "we need to stretch up to achieve this goal"' to my only colleague because he will know full well what I get up to every day, how good I am at my job and what I contribute to the business. It would also be crucial to the success of the business that we understand exactly what we are saying to each other. But dishonesty and the dominance of false perception over reality are as much a part of the furniture of larger offices as photocopiers and piles of A4 paper.

Jargon has traditionally been the language of preference of the business management book, of the Esteemed Guru. It acts again as a dissembling mechanism, hiding the fact that little truly honest, original, insightful or useful is being said. But the time for truth is now surely upon us.

ↄ

The times, they are a-changing

'Truth is like the sun. You can shut it out for a time, but it ain't goin' away.'

Elvis Presley

In July 2001, the first episode of the BBC sitcom *The Office* was aired. The comedy was filmed as a fly-on-the-wall documentary about modern office life, but with no narrator. The central figure was David Brent, played by co-writer Ricky Gervais, who is the jargon-spouting, status-hungry but ultimately insecure and inept manager of a workforce who themselves loaf around not really doing anything in a depressing office of a paper merchant in Slough, west of London.

The show was a resounding success. The second series was viewed by an average of five million viewers in the UK, and the show was snapped up by 25 countries. It sold a million copies on DVD and video, making it Britain's best-selling title ever. It was also a cult success on BBC America, and was the winner of several BAFTAs and even two Golden Globe awards. The character of David Brent himself became an icon among Britain's youth. A 2004 survey found that David Brent was the most popular subject of posters on student walls, defeating traditional favourites such as Martin Luther King, John Lennon and Che Guevara.

The two dominant reactions to the comedy were that it was at once extremely funny and also intensely painful to watch. People laughed hysterically, but often from behind the sofa. It was funny and painful for the same reason. It reflected reality.

Matthew Gilbert of the *Boston Globe* commented that '*The Office* heightens the reality and disconnection of corporate life until it is absurdly funny.' Indeed, much great humour relies on a depiction of a reality which we all recognize, but which we find difficult to confront on a totally serious level. It was George Bernard Shaw who remarked that 'when a thing is funny, search it carefully for a hidden truth.' Outstanding comedy positions itself right at the very intersection between acceptability and taboo. That intersection is indiscernible to the vast majority, hence most attempts at humour are either bland and predictable, or coarse and insensitive. The phrase 'comic genius' is apt because it takes a rare breed of intelligence to locate that very narrow crossover, and thereby avoid mediocrity.

Interestingly, the taboo that lay right at the very surface of the humour of *The Office*, namely the painful reality of office life, had never previously been the central focus of a major sitcom in the UK. The place where many of us spend the majority of the prime years of our lives, and with which we are so familiar, had obviously not been considered a fertile breeding ground for comic writing. After all, there is surely nothing funny in being reminded about misery and boredom, or in seeing our own depressing and useless working lives reflected back to us on our television screens. The fact that *The Office* managed to be so popular is a great testament to the abilities of Ricky Gervais and his co-writer Stephen Merchant in managing to make the taboo subject palatable to audiences.

But nonetheless, pain was unavoidably intertwined with laughter for the viewer. As Bruce Elder of the *Sydney Morning Herald* commented, '*The Office* is painful viewing, but only because the comic creations are so close to reality.'

Indeed they are. Brent is desperate to project an image of modern, innovative leadership and to speak the convoluted language of the business guru, but he ends up sounding like a complete buffoon and antagonizing his subordinates. His deputy, Gareth, is a tactless half-wit, only in his position because he sucks up to Brent and does some of his dirty work for him. Tim is an intelligent sales rep who has an oppressively heightened awareness of the absurdity and mediocrity of his working life, but lacks the gumption to get out of his rut. Dawn is a bored receptionist who harbours ambitions to be an artist, but is trapped in a dull relationship with her Neanderthal boyfriend. The rest of the office staff are seen killing time, trading gossip, staring blankly at their computer screens and looking forward to the drunken release of their next office party. Work itself is a secondary and distant proposition. You can almost smell the stale air of boredom and inertia, of the decaying corpses of the Living Dead.

It's no wonder the nation was watching through its hands. This really was close-to-the-bone stuff. I was reminded of the famous line of the governor in Nikolai Gogol's *Government Inspector*, when he turns to the audience during an amusing scene in the middle of the play and says: 'What are *you* laughing at? You are laughing at yourselves.'

The Office might be the only television sitcom to look at the reality of office life, but other comic depictions are out there. Alex, the *Daily Telegraph* cartoon, which originally began in 1988, features the eponymous merchant banker and his colleague Clive. The American cartoon Dilbert, conceived by Scott Adams in 1989, and very much drawing on his own miserable experience of the corporate world, looks at life in an engineering department of a large company. Both cartoons have spawned several books and in Dilbert's case, an animated television series.

The humour of both cartoons is derived from the ridiculousness of large company life. The characters play the system and indulge in personal battles, but again, the performing of any actual work is not immediately obvious. One reviewer explained Dilbert's popularity in this way: 'Dilbert's success can be traced to its all-too-accurate portrayal of corporate culture as a Kafkaesque world of bureaucracy for its own sake: the boss has power, but no skill; the workers have skills, but no power – and as they learn that their skills are not rewarded, they become mere placeholders who see innovation as dangerous and count anonymity as success.' In other words, Dilbert and his colleagues have come to the same conclusion as many have in the real world of company life – working hard won't necessarily get me anywhere, so why bother?

Another popular comic character is Martin Lukes, invented by *Financial Times* columnist Lucy Kellaway. Lukes is in his forties and is the marketing director of a-b global (UK), a subsidiary of a well-known US multi-national. Kellaway's spoof features e-mails both sent and received by Lukes, who is an ambitious and political company man and a master of meaningless business jargon, sycophancy and astute manoeuvring designed to further his own position. Doing any real work is the last thing on his mind.

The fact that all the above are very popular creations suggests that the taboo subject of our working lives is starting to be breached, albeit generally only in comic form. This feeling was further reinforced by the success of the best-selling French book, *Bonjour Paresse* (Hello Laziness) by Corinne Maier, published in the summer of 2004.

Bonjour Paresse, sub-titled 'the art of doing the least work possible for your employer', is a tongue-in-cheek self-help book urging workers to climb up the company ladder by sitting around not doing anything apart from looking busy. Under chapter headings such as 'The Morons who are sitting next to you', 'Business Culture – my arse', 'Corporate Culture – Stupid People' and 'Why You Can't Lose by Resigning', Maier argues that inaction is a great way to be rewarded in French companies and that do-nothings are frequently promoted into senior management.

Her observations and sarcastic advice to the corporate hopeful are brutal, but only because they carry so much truth: 'Look and sound the part: dress in corporate style and always use meaningless words.' 'Attend all meaningless seminars, motivation weekends, office drinks, works outings, the boss's wife's birthday party.' 'Leave your intellect, personality and imagination at the door and in return the corporate world will look after you so long as you toe the line.' Maier's book met with the predictable response of denial from much of the British media. It merely provided either a welcome excuse to lampoon the 'lazy French', or an opportunity for a sniggering piece on the lifestyle pages about so-called office 'slackers', thus conveniently avoiding any serious discussion of Maier's painfully accurate portrayal of company life.

Stefan Stern, writing in the *Financial Times*, was one of a tiny few who took Maier's message seriously. Bemoaning the fact that no chief executive interviewed had mentioned *Bonjour Paresse* in their nominations for the best recent business management book, Stern wrote: 'It would be interesting to see chief executive officers responding to this critique and facing up to Maier's "active disengagement". The answer to persistently sluggish productivity and poor customer service might be found that way.'

In addition to these artistic and literary signals, there are also clear social indicators that more and more people, not all of them of course suffering from too little to do, are being brave enough to reflect on the true reality of their own working experience. How else do we explain the increasing popularity of the personal life coach? How else do we explain the modern phenomenon of 'downshifting', where people swap corporate life and economic security for something more intrinsically satisfying (2.6 million in the UK and rising rapidly[13])? How else do we explain large numbers of well-paid, successful people leaving their secure jobs to enter the unpredictable and ultimately flawed dot-com industry in the late 1990s? Of course, this modern quest for meaning, excitement and fulfilment, the Zeitgeist of the first decade of this century, has started, as these generational fashions always do, with America and the affluent. But it will, as these things always do, seep gradually into the core mainstream of society.

The above are all signs that employees are becoming increasingly uncomfortable with being dispensable cogs in a faceless machine, and with sitting at their desk-coffin pretending to be occupied or motivated. Tolerance for corporate boredom is starting to wane. The Living Dead, together with people who have other reasons to be dissatisfied with company life, will gradually become less likely to lie to themselves about the reality of their working experience, or maybe even to attempt to hide this reality from their employers. The last taboo is slowly being unearthed, and honesty will in time claim its final scalp, resulting in untold benefits for our economy and for our society. Instead of millions contributing nothing in stagnant workplaces that strip them of their energy and ignore their abilities, those same people will be out in the big wide world contributing something worthwhile. Instead of millions being paid to turn up, those same people will be paid for useful work.

This book is the first attempt to explore the phenomenon of the Living Dead in a completely open, direct and serious way. It will interest anyone anywhere in the world who has ever worked in a large office environment, or those who have a genuine desire to make people's working lives more productive and enjoyable, and hence to see our business culture work more efficiently.

The language used at times in this book might make it seem that I am about to join an anti-globalization demonstration and throw a brick through the window of the nearest McDonald's. This could not be further from the truth. I have indeed a generally low personal opinion of many large companies, but I write this book as a staunch believer in the virtues of the free market. Far from being the vanguard of capitalism, large companies are in fact too often retarding its progress by imprisoning vast oceans of potential.

No matter how hard you look, you will find no jargon in these pages. This is a business book that has nothing to hide.

∽

'Put the key of despair into the lock of apathy. Turn the knob of mediocrity slowly and open the gates of despondency – welcome to the day in the average office.'

David Brent

The second section of this book is devoted to the substantial and wide-ranging effects and consequences of this massive unknown phenomenon, of the stark but unarticulated facts of working life that have been so neatly brushed under the carpet. It will attempt to measure the financial repercussions for individual companies and for the broader economy. It will examine how a society that increasingly values excitement and fulfilment is responding to the Living Dead reality.

The remaining chapters are devoted to explaining the many and various causes of the problem, and to offering potential solutions for those companies that are prepared to open their eyes and confront the reality. (By the way, if you think that the entire phenomenon can be attributed to sheer laziness on the part of the Living Dead, your own lazy mind is about to be challenged. Of course, if you want, you have the option now of closing the book and returning to the cosy fantasy world of work that we have all inhabited for far too long.)

Inefficiency will always eventually be exposed by competition in a free market. That is an inevitable law of economics. The last chapter will look at where the world of office work is headed in the light of the unearthing of the Living Dead. Can large companies reform themselves within their existing fundamental structure, or are we moving gradually towards a completely different type of working model?

But firstly my own experience, which initially prompted my fascination with this whole issue and made me question just how many people must go into an office every day and do extremely little. My story takes the whole Living Death condition to its logical conclusion.

Because my employer forgot for a long while that I even existed.

℘

Notes

1   Vault.com Internet Use Survey, Autumn 2000.
2   Websense Web@Work Survey 2002.
3   Vault.com E-mail Use Survey, Autumn 2000.
4   BBC News website, 21 April 2004.
5   *Insurance Day*, 28 April 2004.
6   *The Scotsman*, 29 April 2004.
7   *Daily Telegraph*, 1 September 2003.
8   BBC News website, 12 April 2000.
9   Reuters, 17 May 2004.
10 BBC News website, 19/1/04.
11 Elle.com/msnbc.com, June 2002.
12 The Times, 9 June 2005.
13 Datamonitor research, April 2003.

CHAPTER 2

MY LIFE IN THE CRACKS

'This little box will be your home for sixty hours a week. It comes with an obsolete computer and a binder about safety hazards. Your challenge is to look busy until someone gives you a meaningful assignment.'

Dilbert

D uring the years 1997 to 2003, I was employed to do a full-time job. If I was to be given now all the work I had to do for my employers during those six years, and I worked hard using all my ability, I would be able to complete all of it very comfortably in about six months, working Monday to Friday, 9 to 5.

One month of work for every year of employment. Sounds about right.

ↂ

21 March 2000

It's a Tuesday afternoon and I am strolling the streets in a beautiful European city, stopping off from time to time at a museum, or a café in a stunning square to watch the world go by. Chatting away to my friend Paul about life, politics, and of course, football. For tonight, we are going to watch Manchester United play in the European Cup in Valencia's Mestalla stadium.

Paul lives in America now and I haven't had the chance to talk to him properly in months.

'Let's get this straight.' He leans forward and I get the impression that he is not going to lean back again until he does get it straight. 'Your company has forgotten about you. You are on their payroll and you don't have to do any work. How long exactly has this been going on?'

'Six months.'

Paul leaned forward further. He wasn't going to let this one go.

'You are getting paid full whack to sit at home doing absolutely f**k all, other than when you don't sit at home doing f**k all because you are going out with your mates or going around Europe watching United?'

'Not a bad summary, although you're forgetting about the cricket and the ...'

'You bastard.'

All the conversations I have had about this period in my life always contain these two words. There is a depressing inevitability about it, although I always enjoy the sneaking respect I sense I get from people for having cheated the system. Except that I wasn't cheating the system. The system was cheating itself.

'When will it end?'

'When they realize, or when I get another job, I suppose.'

Paul was now in a reverie. He was now in the next phase after the 'you bastard' bit, when the other person went through in his mind all the things that he would do if he was being paid, and the company that was paying him was forgetting to get him to fulfil his side of the bargain, like maybe doing some work for them once in a while.

He slowly emerged from his private dream world. 'Full whack to do f**k all ... You bastard.'

Kick-off soon. Better drink up. We clink glasses and we drink to my munificent benefactor, my very own Magwitch, a company we shall refer to for the purposes of this chapter as Humungous plc.

❧

I started working for Humungous, a large insurance company, in London in June 1997. I was employed to try to persuade companies in Russia and the former Soviet Union to insure their assets with us.

I was well qualified for this job. I speak Russian and I had already several years of insurance experience under my belt. I had also been doing exactly the same job for the last two years for another company called Minet (that was the real name). I was leaving Minet to do exactly the same job for Humungous for two reasons. Firstly, Humungous were going to pay me more. Secondly, I was beginning to tire of fat, drunken Russians looking at my Russian language business card, pointing at me while laughing hysterically, and then getting all their friends to look at my card, point at me and laugh hysterically. For 'Minet', in Russian, means 'blow-job'.

Some more sensitive Russians were actually very nice about it and when they referred to Minet in meetings, they would pronounce it rather self-consciously, and with a slight accompanying cough, as 'My Net'. Still, I couldn't help reflecting that the equivalent in English would be introducing me as 'David Bolchover, a representative from the company Blow-Jib'.

According to my dictionary, the translation of the name of my new company was strictly pre-watershed material, so I was pleased that I would now not have to be the butt of so many jokes. Except when fat, drunken Russians pointed at me and said, 'Hey, aren't you the guy who used to work for Blow-job Limited?' and then rolled around laughing.

Within a few months at Humungous, however, I began to get itchy feet. Although I was paid more than I had been previously, I actually had a lot less work to do. Some days, I would just have nothing to do, apart from make the occasional call to Russia. Indeed, it seemed to me that my career since I had graduated from university had gone something like this:

- Small company (PWS) – Quite hard work – Crap money
- Bigger company (Minet) – Less work – More money
- Even bigger company (Humungous) – Even less work – Even more money.

These were the days before the Internet had taken off, so I really was bored when I had nothing to do. Just sitting there for hours staring at the wall, cocooned in my own dream world, with the energy and vitality slowly draining from my body. Going to the coffee machine just to break up the endless spells of nothingness, not because I wanted to drink coffee. Each morning positive and lively, each evening shoulders slumped, head down and mind blunted. I was entering the bleak world of the Living Dead for the first time.

Conversation with colleagues was often my only possible escape from the slow brain-death. Luckily, none of them seemed exactly rushed off their feet either.

There were a couple of Russians and a few public school types working with me. I have always found it quite difficult to connect with the latter. Don't get me wrong, I'm no working-class hero. But growing up as a Jewish boy in Manchester, the only experience I had of countryside and horses was our annual day trip to the Lake District, and the Grand National, when my little brother would put 2p each way on each horse in the race, and then walk around triumphantly for the next week claiming that he had 'won the National'.

So I used to talk to the Russians. They had been brought up in the Soviet Union, and they therefore felt very at ease with life in a large corporate. They were extremely accustomed to listening to meaningless jargon in meetings, observing people trying to ingratiate themselves with those in powerful positions, and avoiding work at all possible costs. In Soviet times, there was a Russian adage that went: 'We pretend to work, and the state pretends to pay us.' No wonder my colleagues loved the West so much. They still pretended to work but this time they actually did get paid with real money, which they could buy things with.

They were not 'new Russians', boring everyone senseless talking about how much they had spent on their latest meal or handbag. They were very much from the old school, and believed that superficial conversation was a long way beneath them. So we whiled away lazy afternoons talking about life, love and fate. I started to think I was like one of the characters in the nineteenth century Russian novels and plays I had read at university, except that I was at my desk in a late twentieth century office in the supposedly buzzing and entrepreneurial City of London, and not in a country dacha sipping tea with Uncle Vanya.

Because the character of the well-educated but ultimately ineffectual man recurred so often in Russian literature of that time, a phrase was coined to describe this personality type – 'lishny chelovek', translated as 'the super-fluous man'. The 'superfluous man' could talk the hind legs off a donkey, and sound pretty impressive to boot, but didn't actually do anything. I was beginning to feel a touch superfluous myself, hence the itchy feet.

I had been working for seven years since leaving university, and I felt I needed a refreshing break from the routine, while giving my career a boost by learning new skills. And as I say, I did not feel that my current position was propelling me at breakneck speed towards the stratosphere of the insurance world.

An MBA seemed the obvious answer. I won a place and a scholarship for half the tuition fees from the Cass Business School. But there was still the other half of the fees and my living costs for the year-long course to think about. I decided to approach Humungous with a proposal – they pay the other half of the fees and a proportion of my current salary as living costs, and I give an undertaking that I shall rejoin the company for a minimum period after the course has ended.

I approached one of my bosses with the idea. I think I had about four bosses at the time, which was great because if you wanted to avoid doing something, you could just say you were working on something for one of the others. And if you wanted to get some money to fund you through an expensive MBA programme, you went to the one who would be most receptive.

In my case, this was the one who was about to retire and just wanted a quiet life. He also sensed that the public schoolboys didn't like me too much and that getting rid of me for a year was a convenient method of avoiding disputes and bad feeling, which would all be very wearisome for him to sort out. He would also have reckoned that when I returned, he would be on some golf course in Spain, and his principal worry would be the choice between sangria and Rioja at the nineteenth hole.

He recommended that the company agree to my suggestion. Once I got his buy-in, the process became a formality. All corporates are keen to demonstrate that they value training and business education for their staff. It is more often than not just lip service, but if those lips were servicing my bank balance, who was I to question the genuineness of their intentions?

So, in September 1998, off I went back to university. As I expected, doing the course endowed me with a renewed energy and optimism. It felt great to make new friendships with people from all over the world and to really stretch myself again, after all those years in the workplace when my brain had been lying in bed all day, only getting up occasionally to sign on at the local brain dole office.

In the midst of the melee of coursework, exams and socializing, the office seemed like a distant memory and an even more distant prospect. But halfway through the year, I popped in to see my retiring boss to remind him that I would be coming back in October. I told him that that the course had given me a real interest in general management and business strategy, and suggested that Humungous should start thinking now about an appropriate position for me which would maximize the return on their investment, rather than just leaving it until I turned up on their doorstep on my first day back.

It was a great speech, full of logic and common sense, but my boss's glazed eyes made him look like an Italian at a cricket match rather than someone who was going to give serious thought to finding a role which would benefit both me and the company. He was in a far away land, somewhere near Marbella, and I had failed miserably to divert his attention away from his sun-drenched villa.

I therefore thought that it might also be a good idea to inform somebody senior in Human Resources of my current situation and what my thoughts were with regard to my next role. The woman I saw nodded and looked interested and said that the necessary wheels would be put in motion.

More months pass and I am now nearing the end of the course. I am still none the wiser about my future and am starting to get a little anxious that my year's hard study would not be rewarded in the way I had expected, not to mention a little angry that nobody at Humungous seems to be assisting me, or even keeping me informed whether there has been any progress in finding me a role. I arranged a meeting with somebody more senior in Human Resources. He predictably knew nothing about me but I gave him the full details. This is the situation, I say, I've done this course, I want this type of job, it's now a month until I'm due to come back, and by the way, don't forget to put me back on full pay on 4 October, as per our agreement. And also, while we're at it, don't expect me to come into the office to sit around twiddling my thumbs, or talking about Turgenev. I'm staying at home until you find something for me to do.

I was fast becoming a 'problem', a buck begging to be passed. I could only imagine what he was thinking: 'Oh shit, I've been landed with this guy at the last minute, he wants to a job in 'strategy' or some bollocks or whatever that is, we owe him a job, he doesn't want his last job back and what's more, those public school types think he's a jumped-up northern Jewboy and wouldn't have him back anyway, so there's no point even persuading him to go back by giving him a load of cock-and-bull about it being temporary before we find him something different. Better pass this one on quick before I start looking like a prize pillock.'

⁂

D-Day, Monday 4 October 1999, arrives. Nothing. A few days later, the HR guy put me in touch with a guy in the finance department, and

I did a couple of days' work for him from home on a project which they soon decided to can. A few weeks pass. Nothing. Apart from, that is, on 26 October when a nice, juicy paycheque was posted through my letterbox.

I am now starting to become accustomed to this lifestyle. After all, it's not every day that somebody effectively pays you to have a great time. Then in mid-November, the finance guy gives me a call. 'There's somebody senior in one of the divisions in London who I think you should meet. His name's Nick and you're bound to like him. He's renowned for finding out just what it is that makes people tick and then slotting them into the right role.'

Which all sounded very impressive, until it emerged that Nick's idea of finding out what made me tick entailed a quick five-minute meeting in his office, and the right role he clearly thought I should be slotted into involved me lying on my sofa reading *Captain Corelli's Mandolin.* In his defence, you could say that Nick was indeed remarkably perceptive about me after such a short meeting, as I would always put reading high up on my list of interests.

Nick set me up with vague meetings with a couple of departments and subsidiaries, but nothing progressed from the initial chat stage. Weeks and months pass with little contact from Nick. I met up with him again at the end of January 2000. He told me that it didn't look as if MBA graduates suited the industry, that there were no obvious opportunities for me at Humungous and they would have to start thinking about making me redundant. I didn't require the debating skills of Alan Dershowitz to suggest that, just maybe, Humungous should have thought about whether MBAs suited the insurance industry before they, as an insurance company, sponsored somebody to go through an MBA course.

I needed to play for time so I could find a job in another company. 'What about a transfer to head office overseas?' I asked. What about this division, what about that department? Come on, you've got 86 zillion employees, surely there must be room for little old me. Nick nodded and agreed to look for more positions in the company, but warned me that I was in 'last chance saloon', which bugged me slightly, because it sounded like a warning and I hadn't done anything wrong.

As it turned out, my last chance saloon was not nearly as scary as it sounded. In fact, I can seriously recommend it to anybody suffering from stress or recuperating from a long illness, anybody that really needs to get away from it all. Especially if you enjoy books, films and going for long walks as much as I do. Because the next time I heard from Humungous was a phone call on 19 July, almost six months, and five whole paycheques, after my last meeting with Nick. And 10 months since I had been put back on full pay. And almost 2 years since I had actually gone into their office to do any work.

How did this happen? I'll tell you how. Because no one individual was in any way bothered about me, no one individual gave me more than two seconds of thought. Because I had fallen through the huge gaping cracks in the system. I had been the object of pass the parcel, and the parcel had been dropped, ignored and then forgotten about.

❧

In the intervening six months, I had been looking for a new job. After a series of interviews, Gargantuan, one of Humungous's competitors, offered me a position to support the chairman of a global division, working on 'business strategy and knowledge management'. I received the offer of employment on 17 July. I was just about to phone Humungous to arrange to come in to say 'hello, remember me, I work for you, I'd like to resign please' when the phone rang to invite me to a meeting with a big chief in the Energy Division.

There is something here that I ought to mention. I had been employed by the Humungous Energy Division throughout. That was the department I had worked in prior to my MBA, which had made the contribution towards the course, and had paid me since I had completed the MBA. When that phone rang to invite me in to the office, it was my first contact with any individual in the Energy Division since I had left for my MBA (if you discount that brief conversation during the course with my distracted and retiring boss). In other words, for almost two years.

I still chuckle when I summon up the vision in my mind of that meeting in the Energy Division that must have taken place when they finally twigged. 'OK guys, we're going to need to cut back on expenditure here, it's never easy, but business is business and it's tough out there and we're all big enough and ugly enough to know that. Why don't we throw a few

ideas on deck and see if they get a tan? Let's look at our payroll first of all
to see if we can let anyone go … OK, let's start at the top … He's too pally
with one of our clients. She's useless but she's got a decent set of knockers
and goes like an absolute choo-choo train … he's a total waste of space,
but isn't he the managing director's nephew? … who in f**k's name is this
guy? David Bolchover? Anyone know him? Does he work here? Bill, for
Christ's sake wake up! Do you know this guy Bolchover?'

After all that time being paid to do nothing for them, it was only right
and proper that they should give me a pay-off to terminate my employment. The big chief walked me to the lifts at the end of the meeting. A
little embarrassed, he asked me what I had been doing for the last few
months. All I could think of was Euro 2000, the Lord's Test, United away
in Europe, sunny afternoons in London zoo, leisurely café breakfasts reading the paper, meeting mates for lunch and the matinee at Screen on the
Hill. Instead, I heard myself utter 'It's obviously been a difficult time for
me and my family'. I didn't have a family.

When the *Sunday Times* does those polls about the best 100 companies
to work for, I always scoff. The top three in 2004 were WL Gore, Beaver-
brooks and Data Connection, who were all selected for their high points
scores from their employees for 'leadership', 'well-being', 'belonging',
'giving back' and 'personal growth'. I have scoured the lists for Humungous
Energy but despite the extremely high rankings I would personally give
them for 'well-being' and 'giving back', they never seem to feature.

⁊

Humungous kept me on their books on full salary for a further month
until mid-August when they eventually gave me the pay-off. So that made
it the best part of 11 months on full pay. It was nice that they gave me the
extra month because I was suffering from yuppie burnout and therefore
needed a break before launching myself into a new challenge.

Was my experience at Humungous a one-off? A freak experience? I
have to tell you that during my subsequent employment at Gargantuan, I
was equally lucky or unlucky, depending on your perspective. Unlucky in
the sense that the work I was given by a mostly absent boss was extremely
uninspiring, and, more pertinently to this debate, was interspersed by long

periods of not having even uninspiring work to do. Lucky in the sense that it gave me the opportunity to research and write my book *The 90-Minute Manager* while sitting at my desk, all paid for by my generous employer.

My career, including titles, can therefore be updated as follows:

- Small company (PWS) – No Title – Quite hard work – Crap money
- Bigger company (Minet) – Divisional Director – Less work – More money
- Even bigger company (Humungous) – Assistant Vice-President (practically up there with Dick Cheney) – Even less work and including 11 months of doing literally no work – Even more money
- Another very big company (Gargantuan) – Director – Very little work, apart from writing a book – Still more money

❧

The frightening thought that has been churning through my mind during the last few years is that I could have gone through my whole career quite comfortably doing very little and earning quite a decent amount of cash, thank you very much. OK, I would have had to make a little more effort hiding the fact that I was doing very little, but that would by no means have been beyond the realms of my intelligence and cunning.

I have looked around my own offices and have seen a lot of people doing very little for much of the time. I have also seen a lot more people trying to look as if they are doing something when anyone observing them with a modicum of perceptiveness would realize that they were actually doing nothing. My more recent honesty about my own experience has helped to induce similar stories from people I have met outside work.

This book is not about Humungous, Gargantuan or me. Those are the companies I just happened to work for. Large numbers of people right across the industry spectrum apparently manage to endure the Living Death existence through much of their working lives, and sometimes even receive large compensation for it. (By the way, that word 'compensation' in relation to salary, often used in job advertisements, has always fascinated me. Compensation quite clearly indicates payment in return for a negative experience. The word therefore offers a glimmer of honesty in the dishonest world of white-collar office work: 'You waste your life getting bored in a soulless office and we'll make it worth your while.')

Stories about all these people getting paid to do very little might appear amusing to the dispassionate observer. But for shareholders of individual companies and for anyone who cares about the fate of the broader economy, the Living Dead are no laughing matter.

೧೨

CHAPTER 3

MONEY FOR NOTHING

'I had persuaded myself that actually I probably did roughly the same amount of work as many men my age, namely around two or three hours a day. But I was determined that I wouldn't waste the rest of my life pretending to be working, flicking my computer screen from solitaire to a spreadsheet, or suddenly changing the tone of personal phone calls when the managing director walked into the office. From what I could gather from my contemporaries, there were a lot of jobs where you arrived in the morning, chatted for an hour or two, did some really useful work between about eleven and lunchtime, came back in the afternoon, sent a stupid e-mail message to Gary in accounts before spending the rest of the afternoon in apparent total concentration while downloading a picture of a naked transsexual from http://www.titsandcocks.com'.

Michael Adams, in The Best a Man Can Get by John O'Farrell

H ave you ever worked in a large office and asked yourself: 'What do those people in that corner over there *actually* do? I know what their formal job titles or roles are. But what do they *actually* do?' Or have you ever got chatting to someone about their job, delved a little deeper than the superficial 'what do you do?' and at the end of the conversation were none the wiser about what their work *actually* entailed.

All these people wondering what others really do every day to earn their living. But then, putting those ideas to the back of their mind and not really thinking about them again. After all, it's not very important to them as individuals what somebody else does or doesn't do. And anyway, those other people must really be frightfully busy, because their job titles sound so grand and I heard this professor on the radio this morning saying that the British population will be extinct by 2050 because of overwork and stress.

Put all these isolated thoughts and conversations together into a collective whole and we start to piece together the truth about what is really happening. The chances are that if another person's declared details of their everyday activities sound unconvincing or vague, and they don't work for a very small company, they probably don't do very much. But because we are not following that person around all day, we assume the best and the most glamorous about their working lives, and imagine that like everyone else appearing on the television, they must be frantically juggling their work/life balance issues until they finally succumb to the twin inevitabilities of alcoholism and erectile dysfunction.

We ourselves might do very little in our jobs for long periods, but that's just us, isn't it? We're not normal. It's not widespread. The bloke opposite me at work never does anything – whenever I walk past his desk, he's on some car website or playing computer golf. But that's just our small section of our department that allows that to happen. Our boss doesn't care, he's never around. But over there, it must be different. And whenever I go upstairs to another department, they are always rushing around, walking purposefully and talking quickly, as if they are conducting the final phase of an SAS-style military operation.

As frequently is the case in corporate life, flimsy and lazy perception of others can too easily eclipse hard reality. And the reality exposes the huge waste, the farce, of paying people to go through the motions, to occupy a position for a certain number of hours, rather than for the work that they produce.

The employment drain

The old-style, traditional pursuits of the Living Dead – chatting with colleagues, staring out of the window or shuffling papers – have now been joined by more modern techniques for passing the hours in the working day. Devastatingly for the media-inspired image of an overworked workforce, these techniques are also often a great deal more measurable.

You can now do a realistic job of estimating the actual cost of non work-related activities in the office (I deliberately shy away from using popular terms like shirking or slacking because much of the time, workers won't have any real work to shirk from). The huge inefficiencies and, surely, the long-term inviability of traditional office culture, are there for all to see.

The employee Internet management company Websense attempted to calculate the financial cost of the time spent by US employees surfing Internet sites which had absolutely nothing to do with their job. Employees surveyed admitted spending 1.5 hours per week visiting such sites. Even if we take this figure at face value (any Internet-savvy office employee saying that they only spend 1.5 hours on the web at work all week should by rights elicit the 1970s schoolboy response of the stroked chin and the loud utterance of the words 'Jimmy Hill'), its financial repercussions are massive. Websense multiplied this figure by the average US salary, as reported by the US Bureau of Labor Statistics, and by the number of employees with access to the Internet (70 million). They concluded that the resulting loss to US industry was a whopping $85 billion per annum, which was approximately the GDP of one of the Asian economic tigers, Singapore, in the year of the survey, 2002.

Suspicious minds might argue that a company such as Websense, which sells software that limits employee access to certain non-work related sites, has a vested interest in producing alarming statistics such as these. But Websense actually took a conservative line. They accepted the figure of 1.5 hours per week as admitted by the employees, and ignored the far more realistic estimate of 8.3 hours (more than one working day per week) proffered by company HR managers in their survey, which was presumably based on some hard evidence of their employees' everyday online activities. If we take the latter figure, we are talking the small matter of a loss to US industry of $470 billion, which is getting us up to the total GDP of Brazil.

Another company, Internet Policy Consulting, came up with a compromise figure. Using its own research and that of several other organizations, it estimated in 2003 that the US economy would lose approximately 10 billion hours in productive workplace time during that year because of employee usage of the Internet. The company estimated the cost to the economy at $250 billion. After the release of the report, Internet Policy said: 'The 10 billion lost working hours is the equivalent to 5 million office workers being paid to web surf for an entire year,' i.e. America, through the goodness of its heart, ships the population of Scotland over for a year and pays them to sit around viewing www.celticfc.co.uk and www.billyconnolly.com.

In the UK, a 2002 survey by Cranfield School of Management found that 30% of the small and medium size companies questioned were losing more than a day's work per week to Internet surfing and personal e-mail use, costing this sector of the economy an estimated total of £1.5 billion per year. The impact on individual company profit margins was far-reaching. According to the report, a company that makes £700,000 profit on a turnover of £10–12 million could be losing 15% of its profits due to non work-related web and e-mail use.

If so much waste is prevalent in smaller companies, then we can only speculate about the cost of waste in Britain's larger companies (no similar survey has been conducted on them), where hiding in the cracks will be so much easier. Indeed, the less conspicuous you are, the more likely you will be to abuse your workplace Internet connection. According to a 2002 *Personnel Today* survey, 57% of the Human Resource personnel interviewed said that employees with their own offices were the most guilty of such abuse.

In the absence of published data, let's do our own maths on this. If we take a larger company with a workforce of 5000, and apply the 2003 UK average hourly wage of £12.03, ignore significant employee overheads and take a conservative line on Internet usage per week, say 5 hours on average, the total annual loss to that company will still be more than £14 million. And if we expand this calculation for the working population as a whole (7.1 million British workers had workplace Internet access by the end of 2003), the loss to UK plc is more than £20 billion per year, even after the input of such cautious data. To put this loss in some sort of perspective, the annual government expenditure on defence is around £30 billion and the NHS received £82 billion in 2004.

And 5 hours does appear to be a low estimate. Some workplace Internet usage statistics appeared in Chapter 1 but here are a few more, just to be getting on with:

- News websites reach 35.5% more users at work than at home, and work users also spent 68% longer on these sites (understandable, there's stuff to do at home). (*Nielsen/Net Ratings*)
- 31% more users surf finance sites at work rather than at home, spending 102% more time on these sites (come on, a man has to earn a living!) (*Nielsen/Net Ratings*)
- 46% of holiday online shopping takes place at work. (*Nielsen/Net Ratings*)
- In December 2002 in the United States, 7.9 million workplace Internet users viewed personals sites (online dating), with the at-work users accounting for 35% of the time spent on such sites (must be useful for those rare occasions when you can't find anyone at work who will get down and dirty with you). (*eMarketer*)
- 74% of online radio listening occurs between 5 a.m. and 5 p.m. on weekdays, while only 14% occurs at the weekend (never tried that one – missed out there. Just one inconspicuous ear-piece and the day must just fly by). (*Streaming Media World*)
- 23% of French employees admit to using the Internet for more than an hour per day for personal reasons. Around 72% of those who use the net for personal use admitted that they go online during company time rather than during lunch breaks or after work hours. Only 3% of survey respondents claimed that they never use the Internet for personal use at work. (*The Benchmark Group*)

- 64% of US office employees say that they use the net for personal interest during working hours. This is divided as follows: 26% less than an hour a day, 22% one to two hours, 8% three to four and another 8% spend more than five hours on personal net use (so much for the lazy French). (*Greenfield Online*)
- The average US employee spends 75 minutes a day making personal use of company technology such as phones, computers, fax machines and copiers. (*Gallup*)
- Almost 40% of workers in the UK, Germany and the US spend an hour or more every day e-mailing their friends and relatives via their company e-mail system during working hours. In a typical 100-person company, according to Clearswift, almost 1700 working days each year are lost because people are using corporate e-mail systems for non-company purposes, equivalent to taking on 7 new full-time staff. (*Clearswift*)
- The average US worker wastes 2 hours a day. 44% said their No. 1 method of wasting time at work is personal internet use. (America Online and Salary.com)

Many of these workplace Internet statistics involve employees' own estimation of their own activities. We could easily take an appropriately cynical view, and conclude that workers on average will tend to play down the amount of time they spend not working, for the benefit of their own self-image as much as anything. We could instead look at the amount of time a worker spends on the Internet in total, and then make our own approximate conclusions about how he divides this time. Nielsen/Net Ratings, a company that measures Internet usage, reported that office workers in the United States spent an average of 21 hours and 41 minutes a week online in November 2003. How many office jobs require anywhere near that amount of Internet work? And anyway, much work-related Internet usage will involve the quick and easy accessing of information from well-known websites, not time-consuming surfing, chatting and in-depth reading.

This is clearly not just a case of stretched employees relaxing for a few minutes in between pressing assignments (although it will be for some). This is a large-scale structural problem. A myriad of websites and chatrooms have sprung up specifically to cater for the millions of workplace Internet users seeking to fill out their days, once they get bored of their favourite sports and shopping sites. www.Ishouldbeworking.com, which attracts more than 10,000 visitors a day, posts a weekend countdown on its main page and has handy tools for 'office loafers', including a program to guard your privacy online and a download that makes it look as if your computer is running a test or installation, while you go off for a coffee break. Other popular sites include www.slackersguild.com, www.boredatwork.com and www.donsbosspage.com, which offers tips on stealth-like surfing at work, provides panic/protector buttons to help you cover your tracks if your manager is coming, and also has sound clips of busy office activity just in case your boss can't see what you're doing but has a habit of eavesdropping. www.ihatework.co.uk, which promotes a mid-week discount offer to visit Alton Towers, was set up after the theme park discovered that one in three of their visitors had given false excuses to their employer to take time off.

Indeed, you can only waste time in the office if you are actually there. Total workplace absence in the UK in 2003 was 176 million days, an average of 7.2 days per employee. According to 500 private companies polled by the CBI and Axa Insurance, 15% (and the rest!) of all this sickness absence, 25 million days, were the result of 'sickies', where employees feign illness to take time off. The cost of covering the salaries of absent staff was £11.6 billion (£475 per employee), including £1.75 billion for the alleged dishonest absence. 78% of the companies said there was either a definite or possible link between patterns of absence and the unauthorized extension of the weekend (i.e. not surprisingly, a disproportionate percentage of workplace absence is on a Friday or Monday). A 2005 survey on sick days by Peninsula, the employment law firm, proved this conclusively. Monday and Friday were shown to be the days most commonly taken as sick (23% and 25% respectively) whereas Wednesday is the most rarely taken (8%).

Tellingly, larger organizations reported much higher absence levels than smaller ones. In the public sector, the absenteeism rate is 10.1 days per employee. Private firms employing over 5000 averaged a similar figure, 10.2 days per employee, while companies with less than 50 staff averaged only 4.2 days. This large organization absenteeism has been very evident at British Airways. Staff there take, on average, 16.7 days a year off sick, or three and a half working weeks, costing the company £60 million. The CBI believes smaller firms have lower absence rates because of more frequent senior management contact and greater peer pressure. If you apply the same logic to workplace Internet usage in large companies, then the figures, when they do come out, will be frightening. Indeed, it's no wonder they *haven't* come out. If 30% of small to medium companies say they are losing a full day or more per week to personal online use, many larger companies must be jealously guarding their own statistics for fear of a loss of customer and shareholder confidence if they ever seep into the public sphere.

Alcohol is to blame for much of workplace absence and lack of productivity. According to a 2004 survey by employment agency Reed, hangovers cost the UK economy £2.8 billion per year (the UK government overseas aid budget for 2004 was £3.8 billion, £4.4 billion being reserved for the wars in Iraq and Afghanistan). Ten million working days are lost annually through alcohol excess, costing British business an estimated £960 million, when staff take days off sick through being too hung over to work (again, this is a conservative estimate – the government's own strategy unit estimated annual alcohol-related sick-days at 17 million).

In addition, Reed reported that hungover employees blight a further 72 million working days a year, with workers turning up to work, on average, two and a half days a year when hungover. Employees estimate their hangovers cause only a 27% loss in productivity when they do bother to turn up (they must still have been hammered when they came up with this figure), which still equates to a total loss of 19 million working days annually and an additional cost to UK business of £1.8 billion in lost working hours. Similar studies have estimated the annual cost of hangovers in the workplace in Australia at US$3.8 billion and in the United States at a massive US$148 billion.

24-hour pub opening, scheduled to start in the UK in 2005, is a boon for personal liberty, but will surely further reduce productivity, especially in companies with a younger workforce. As mentioned in Chapter 1, an informal survey carried out by two graduates in their twenties of more than 500 friends, acquaintances and colleagues found that a third of young professionals are hungover at least twice a week on working days. 55% of these aged between 18 and 25 interviewed in the Reed survey believed that 24-hour licences will adversely affect workplace productivity.

According to certain sections of the workforce surveyed by Reed, acceptability of hangovers in the workplace is also on the increase. In response to the question, 'do you think it is more acceptable to turn up for work with a hangover than it was three years ago', 31% of employees thought it was more acceptable. Unsurprisingly, the percentage who think that it is more acceptable is highest amongst administrative and support staff and graduate trainees (those more likely to have the hangovers), while the percentage who think that it is less acceptable is highest amongst managers and directors (remote figures with little idea what is going on beneath them).

℘

Obvious methods of measuring workplace inefficiency are illuminating, but do not represent the complete picture. Personal Internet use, for instance, has simply *augmented* the tools a bored worker would have had in his armoury in the pre-Internet days to waste time until the final whistle of the working day. It has not replaced them. People will still chat for long periods with colleagues about non work-related issues, nip out 'for a meeting', go to the toilet and come back an hour later, or dream the day away thinking about those future times when they won't have to spend eight or more hours a day doing something that robs them of their zest for life, unless of course they are dead by then.

So how can we put a figure on the cost of more invisible non-work activities? Rather than look at the measurable result of workplace disinterest, we could turn the logic around and attempt to estimate the number of employees who are completely demotivated by their jobs and then make assumptions about the (non) work activities that would be the inevitable consequence of their out-and-out lack of interest.

Gallup conducts regular research into worker motivation through its *Employee Engagement Index* Q12 surveys. The Q12 comprises twelve questions given to individual employees such as: 'At work, do I have the opportunity to do what I do best every day?' 'At work, do my opinions seem to count?' and 'Does my supervisor, or someone at work, seem to care about me as a person? In its analysis of the results of its survey, Gallup divides employees into three types – the 'engaged' (loyal, productive, find their work satisfying), the 'not engaged' (not psychologically committed to their roles and may leave if an opportunity presents itself) and the 'actively disengaged' (disenchanted with their workplaces). The 'actively disengaged' is possibly the nearest technical term we have to 'The Living Dead'; that is, people who are totally emotionally disconnected from their work. According to Gallup, the 'actively disengaged' are 'significantly less productive' and are absent from work 3.5 days a year more on average than other workers. Psychologically, Gallup says, they have already left their jobs.

For its first US survey in 2001, Gallup found that 26% were 'engaged', 55% 'not engaged' and 19% of the workforce (24.7 million workers) were 'actively disengaged'. The cost of the low productivity, absenteeism and high employee turnover of the 'actively disengaged' section of the workforce was estimated at between \$292 billion and \$355 billion a year. A similar survey in Britain revealed 19% 'engaged', 61% 'not engaged' and 20% 'actively disengaged'. The cost to the economy was estimated at between £37.2 billion and £38.9 billion (puts defence spending in the shade, then). In Germany, only 12% were 'engaged' and 18% were 'actively disengaged', the annual loss being estimated at up to €260 billion. France had the highest proportion of 'actively disengaged' workers at 21%.

In all surveys, a significant majority was uninspired at work and a significant minority just didn't want to be there at all. Millions go to their office every day on sufferance simply to earn a wage, where they hide from view, whiling the days away doing the very minimum necessary to remain in roles that produce little and cost tens and hundreds of billions. The equally unproductive contribution of many more employees, the scheming and Machiavellian Professional Operators, who are discussed in detail in Chapter 5, is no doubt lost in such surveys. They quite possibly feature among 'the engaged', relishing spending their days immersed in the political challenge of forming astute strategic alliances and climbing to the high reaches of the corporate world, where they can reap boundless financial rewards and bask in the adulation of ambitious underlings.

Far from being the ruthlessly streamlined, rapacious profitmongers portrayed by sections of the political left, many large companies are in fact still bedevilled by huge inefficiencies and suffer from widespread institutional waste. They don't just tolerate large-scale inactivity, they pay hand over fist for it. And as for our economy as a whole, it loses out twice over. Firstly, because companies sacrifice so much of their profitability forking out for non-productivity. Secondly, because of the massive opportunity cost. Millions of unproductive people are not being forced out of their cushy, salaried hiding place to contribute their resourcefulness, talents and energies in a less stultifying environment, which counters personal drift and pushes them to achieve. People may feel bored and lifeless in their jobs, but it's too easy for them to stay put for too long, psychologically trapped by cosy financial security. And all the while using the minimal ingenuity required to fool their bosses into believing that they serve a useful commercial purpose (not that most of the bosses care whether they do or don't).

Necessity is the mother of all invention. Because so many currently unproductive people do not feel that necessity – the economy and society lose out hugely on vital sources of creativity and innovation.

The economic six-pointer

When two football teams fighting relegation play against each other, the game is often known as a 'six-pointer'. The team that wins the game takes three points, and just as importantly deprives the rival team of three valuable points, hence the value of six points notionally attributed to the game. In the economic game between waste and productivity, every employee not doing very much within the warm environment of salaried work hands a 'six-pointer' to Team Waste.

Rather than just being paid to turn up, workers could be out in the big wide world seeking to get paid for producing something useful or worthwhile. Inevitably, as any freelance contractor, individual entrepreneur or small company start-up would tell you, this is no simple exercise. It often requires huge effort, passion, enterprise and imagination to make it work. All of which are more conducive to social and economic progress than the stagnant inertia of large office life.

Incentive is key. The sole trader or start-up business must offer something that others want to buy in order to survive and prosper. The large company employee has no such incentive to innovate, to plug gaps in the market, to fashion progress. He gets paid whatever he does. The upside, the potential gain, of thinking up new ideas is limited. As soon as he does, flocks of Professional Operators, feathers rustled by the threat of the upstart, swoop from nowhere to attach themselves to the idea in order to appropriate any available glory. Indira Gandhi, the former prime minister of India, recalled her grandfather's advice: 'He once told me that there were two kinds of people: those who do the work and those who take the credit (Grandpa Gandhi clearly hadn't heard of the Living Dead, who do neither). He told me to try to be in the first group; there was much less competition.'

Financially, too, the corporate innovator doesn't have much to gain. A possible percentage increase here, a possible inflated bonus there – that's if he's very lucky. And what about the downside? Creativity jeopardizes the status quo, and therefore all the people who profit from it. Thinking and acting outside company norms places the inventive head above the parapet, and exposes him to the revenge of powerful others. The lessons are soon learned, extinguishing youthful initiative and independent thought. Know your place, play the game, wait your turn, make the right friends. The ironic advice of Corinne Maier is soon understood and obeyed: 'Bear in mind that trying to change the system is futile'.

You can always rely on someone else to do the working and the thinking anyway. There are thousands of people here, for God's sake, I'll take it easy today, a few too many last night, I'm afraid, you know how it is. The smaller the company, the faster the buck stops, the more you have to act to survive. The greater the sense of individual responsibility and necessity, the speedier and more effective the response.

This is convincingly demonstrated by research conducted in the 1960s by two American psychologists, Bibb Latané and John Darley. Their research was prompted by an infamous murder case. In 1964, on her way home from work, a woman named Kitty Genovese was attacked in Queens, New York. 38 of her neighbours, awakened by her screams, watched from their apartment windows as her assailant took more than half an hour to murder her. No one called the police.

This murder, as all murders in similar circumstances have done since, sparked outrage and shame within society. Latané and Darley subsequently conducted a series of studies to attempt to explain what they termed the 'bystander problem'. They simulated various mock emergencies in different situations in order to gauge how many would come to help, and in what circumstances. They found that the one factor above all else that predicted helping behaviour was how many witnesses there were to the event.

In one experiment, for example, Latané and Darley asked a student who was alone in a room to stage an epileptic fit. When the other research subjects each thought they were the only one able to hear the distressed student, 85% of them went to seek help from the researchers. When subjects thought two others heard the seizure, only 62% went for help. And when they thought five others heard the seizure, only 31% went for help. In another experiment, people who saw smoke coming from under a doorway would report it 75% of the time when they were on their own, but the incident would be reported only 38% of the time when they were in a group. From such studies, Darley and Latané concluded that bystander inaction is caused primarily by the diffusion of responsibility. When other people are present to share the burden of responsibility, we feel less compelled to act. In the words of Malcolm Gladwell, in his book *The Tipping Point*, 'the lesson is not that no one called despite the fact that 38 people heard her (Genovese) scream; it's that no one called *because* 38 people heard her scream. Ironically, had she been attacked on a lonely street with just one witness, she might have lived.'

℮℈

The most alert, responsive and creative unit of human endeavour is the lone individual. When surrounded by too many others, that individual does not feel the pressure to react to a situation or to perform to the utmost of his ability. He leaves it to others to exert themselves. The trouble is, pretty much everyone else is thinking the same thing. Dispersed responsibility breeds collective apathy, whereas individual accountability and necessity spur action.

And that logic accounts for the huge benefits which entrepreneurial activity confers on the economy and society. As *The Economist* put it in 2004: 'For much of industrial history, small firms have been responsible for the bulk of breakthrough products. The Small Business Administration, which seeks to promote the interests of small businesses in the United States, claims that the pacemaker, the personal computer, the Polaroid camera and pre-stressed concrete all emerged from small entrepreneurial outfits, and those are taken only from the list of items beginning with the letter P.'

Entrepreneurs indeed do lead the way in developing ideas. They are responsible for the bulk of innovation: 67% of inventions, according to the Global Entrepreneurship Monitor, and 95% of radical innovations since the Second World War, according to Jeffry Timmons in his book *New Venture Creation*. As the management writer Peter Drucker notes in his book *Innovation & Entrepreneurship*: 'Entrepreneurs see change as the norm and as healthy. Usually they do not bring about the change themselves. But – and this defines entrepreneur and entrepreneurship – the entrepreneur always searches for change, responds to it and exploits it as an opportunity.'

This perpetual quest for opportunity, and the resulting innovation, translate into growth, prosperity and jobs. The Global Entrepreneurship Monitor (GEM) Report, inaugurated in the late 1990s, is an annual assessment within selected countries of the national level of entrepreneurial activity, defined as 'any attempt at new business or new venture creation'. Its broad purpose is to measure the magnitude of entrepreneurial activity as well as the impact such activity has on economic growth. It has found a very strong correlation of 0.7 (1 is a perfect positive correlation, –1 is a perfect negative correlation) between the level of entrepreneurial activity in a given country and economic growth. The surveyed countries that have high levels of entrepreneurial activity all have above-average levels of economic growth. More than half of the gross domestic product of the world's richest country, the United States, is accounted for by small business (defined as having fewer than 500 employees).

New and small firms are the major source of new jobs in a changing economy. Jeffry Timmons asserts that although Fortune 500 companies in the United States jettisoned more than 5 million jobs between 1980 and 1998, more than 34 million new jobs were added to the economy in the same period, most of which were created by entrepreneurs and small business. According to small business expert and former Harvard lecturer, David Birch, large firms lost two million jobs between 1994 and 1998 in the United States, while small firms created ten million jobs. Whereas larger companies will gradually outsource more of their functions, 80% of entrepreneurs worldwide expect to create jobs once their companies are more established, and about 20% expect to create twenty or more jobs (Global Entrepreneurship Monitor). In a review by the Organization for

Economic Cooperation and Development (OECD) of studies from ten countries, 13 out of the 16 studies found that job creation fell as the size of a company increased. Larger companies tend to expand only through take-overs.

There are two types of entrepreneur identified by the GEM; one driven by desire (the 'pull factor'), the other by necessity (the 'push factor'). The first type, the energetic, imaginative, born entrepreneur is unlikely to spend too much time, if any, in a large corporate, before getting sick of the posturing, and starting to yearn for action and progress. Certain cultures produce this breed of entrepreneur more than others, and the UK lags behind in this regard. Aversion to the risk of setting up and running a new business is relatively high, and the role of the entrepreneur is literally not half as respected and acclaimed as it is in North America. The 1999 GEM Study found 91% of US entrepreneurs and 88% of Canadian entrepreneurs agreeing that 'starting a business is a respected occupation'. Only 38% of their UK counterparts agreed (a pitiful 8% of Japanese agreed, which goes a long way to explaining their recent economic problems). Consequently, Britain had only about 3.5 business start-ups per 100 people of working age in 1999, compared with more than 8 per 100 in the US. And this culture is self-perpetuating. The GEM 2003 report found that people who know someone who started a business in the past six months are two to three times more likely to engage in entrepreneurial activity themselves.

The second type of entrepreneur, those who need to set up a business just to subsist and prosper, are still far too rare. It's still far easier to hide in a large office, and pick up a nice pay cheque every month, than to run a sustainable business. But the inexorable march of competition will gradually and inevitably expose the gross inefficiencies of large companies, certainly at the very least leading to an increasing proportion of people being employed by newer, smaller and more dynamic operations. Fortunately, modern society is beginning to strengthen the 'pull factor' too, by means of its quest for individual fulfilment and excitement, and its impatience with humdrum routine.

∽

CHAPTER 4

THE QUEST FOR MEANING

'The Office is about lack of ambition. If you're not happy, don't suddenly wake up when you're 65 and think: 'Oh, I should have left. I wanted to be an artist.'

'It's OK for a couple of years to have a lovely, cozy job, but you don't want to wake up at 60 and go, aw, f**k, I was gonna write a book. Shit, I forgot. I was drinkin' in a bar with all my mates, but they wrote books. F**k. That's the terrible thing.'

Ricky Gervais, co-writer, The Office, BBC comedy

N o one on their deathbed wishes they had spent more time in the office. Any office worker, no matter how senior or successful, would surely be lying if they denied the immense power of this one sentence. And with each generation that passes, we reflect on its significance more and more.

Increased wealth in our societies is not producing a corresponding increase in happiness. If a person is very poor, there is no doubt that greater income can improve his or her life. But once the basics are secured, well-being does not necessarily correlate with wealth. Findings from the World Values Survey, an assessment of life satisfaction in more than 65 countries conducted between 1990 and 2000, indicate that income and happiness tend to grow at similar rates only until about US$13,000 of annual income per person (calculated at 1995 purchasing power parity). After that, additional income appears to yield only modest increments in self-reported happiness.

Economic well-being might not make us happier, but it does make us think much more about whether we are happy or not. Modernity stimulates introspection. Despite the fact that the media harp on about how busy we all are, we reflect more on our own lives than ever before. We constantly question what we are doing; we don't just accept it because it happens to have been the norm.

Financial security means we no longer worry about putting food on the table for our children, generations of men are growing up without the real threat of being sent off to war, and religion and the prospect of divine retribution no longer concentrate our minds in the same way. But the human propensity for anxiety, built up over millennia, does not just disappear. It has to go somewhere. And it has reoriented itself to focus on the self.

A negative consequence of this phenomenon has been the dramatic increase in rates of depression. The number of Americans treated for depression soared from 1.7 million to 6.3 million between 1987 and 1997, and the proportion of those receiving antidepressants doubled. A study released in 1988 found that Americans born after 1945 were 10 times more likely to suffer from depression than people born 50 years earlier. Another study from 1991 produced results indicating a similar trend. Of Americans born before 1955, only one per cent had suffered a major depression; of those born after 1955, six per cent had become depressed by age 24.

More wealth and more luxury goods just seem to make us want more of what money can't buy. In 1968, the psychologist Abraham Maslow wrote the classic *Toward a Psychology of Being*, which systematized the evolution of human needs. In Maslow's hierarchy of five basic needs, the individual does not feel the second need until the demands of the first have been satisfied, nor the third until the second has been satisfied, and so on. The needs are as follows: physiological (food, water etc.), security (shelter, removal from danger), belonging (love, affection, being part of a group), esteem (self-esteem and status) and lastly, self-actualization (achievement of individual potential).

Maslow describes the pinnacle of the pyramid of needs, self-actualization, as a person's need to be and do that which the person was 'born to do'. 'A musician must make music, an artist must paint, and a poet must write if they are ultimately to be at peace with themselves. What humans can be, they must be.' Ignoring needs for self-actualization results in restlessness, a sense that something, possibly indefinable to that person, is missing.

And as there's not too much self-actualizing going on in your average office, apart from maybe in the gents' lavatories on particularly slow days, the corporate world faces an escalating challenge. If the advance of modernity is constantly expanding people's horizons beyond material possessions and status, how will the workplace be affected? Fifty years ago, stoical workers grateful for peace, freedom and an end to food rations, and still mindful of the depression of the 1930s, might have anticipated and accepted workplace boredom in their pursuit of economic security. But in fifty years from now? Will this trade-off, boredom for security, be tolerable to the majority then? A mighty clash is already under way. Large office life versus modern life. And if the pools' panel were sitting, it would surely plump for an away win.

The restless age

Several books have recently been published focusing on the 'quarterlife crisis', detailing the emotional and career challenges facing people in the early stages of their career. This is not just a populist fad. Looking at surveys of the attitude of that generation towards their work, 'crisis' does not seem too strong a word. This is a generation that believes itself imprisoned, and spends days dreaming of tunnels and Steve McQueen-style getaways.

A 2003 survey, carried out by the communications agency Fish Can Sing, revealed that 67% of employees aged between 18 and 35 in the UK are 'unhappy at work', including 83% of 30–35 year-olds. 63% of those aged between 30 and 35 say they felt work was a 'disappointment'; that it had not lived up to their expectations. One in fifteen of those interviewed had already left what they described as a conventional career job in favour of something they found to be more rewarding, such as charity work, outdoors employment or creative occupations. A further 45% were considering a similar change. Most of the disillusioned said that stress was the major reason for wanting to leave, with boredom and lack of fulfilment following closely behind. The report also noted, tellingly, that in the past decade the number of young people who fear 'dying without achieving anything' has doubled to 65%.

A survey from 2004 by the UK Teacher Training Agency found that almost one in three graduates is bored at work and wants to change careers. Almost half complained of a lack of 'intellectual challenge'. More than one third of those entering teacher training are now 'career changers' over the age of 30. The government advertising campaign to recruit teachers makes a deliberate attempt to capitalize on the boredom felt by so many. 'Use your head. Teach.' is its slogan.

Another study from 2004 by Common Purpose, a leadership development organization, concluded that 83% of young professionals aged from 25 to 35 believed themselves to be in the midst of a 'quarterlife crisis'. Nearly half of respondents felt 'stuck' in a career, but had amassed too many debts to leave. Nearly nine out of ten said that they were seeking careers that fulfilled their potential, as well as adding a sense of 'purpose' to their lives, and 59% said that their current employment did not provide this fulfilment. The group as a whole complained of being treated like 'corporate machines' at their workplace and felt that their office achievements offered no value to the real world.

A survey conducted at the beginning of 2004 found that a whopping seven in ten Irish workers hope to make a fresh start in the new year by changing career. According to the results of the survey, only 27% of respondents would choose the same career again given the opportunity to turn the clock back. Personal fulfilment was the biggest influence on their decision to change career (53%).

These statistics are quite staggering, given the inevitable propensity of many to deny the full extent of the reality of their working lives to themselves and to others. People, especially those with ambition, don't like admitting even to themselves that their working lives are a 'disappointment'. After all, their work forms the majority of their waking hours and the basis still for how they are judged by many in society. So let's bump up those percentages a little further, shall we?

As the first survey indicated, some are not just dreaming of tunnels. They are actually burrowing through them, or have even come out the other side. Downshifting, the practice of opting to earn less in return for a life deemed to be more satisfying, is rapidly gaining pace. According to Datamonitor, a business information and research company, 200,000 British workers will have downshifted in 2004, bringing the total to about 3 million overall, a sharp hike from about 1.7 million in 1997. The company predicts that their number will reach 3.7 million by 2007, part of a movement of around 12 million across Europe. Similar research in Australia shows that nearly one person in four between the ages of 30 and 60 has, in the past 10 years, taken the downshifting path by switching lifestyle or career paths or stopping work altogether, in exchange for a better lifestyle. The insurance company Prudential concludes from its own research that one in 14 British workers has already downshifted and that more than half a million 35 to 54-year-olds plan to join them in the next three years. Angus McIver, the company's director of research, acknowledges the noteworthy scale of this rejection of the traditional career path: 'An alarming number of people appear to be unhappy in their employment and unfulfilled by their work.'

The downshifters are often watched avidly with deep envy by those still trapped in their corporate Colditz, or with intense *schadenfreude* by those same people if the escape was ill-conceived and poorly executed ('Ha! Just look at those naïve fools. What *were* they thinking of? Life isn't a bed of roses, you know. Bet they're regretting they jacked in their company pension now'). The proliferation of television programmes such as Channel 4's *No Going Back* or *A Place in the Country*, which track the fortunes of downshifters, caters for this new voyeurism. This is fantasy television, teasing bored workers with glimpses of what their one and only life could be like if only they gave it a chance. It gives them that 'first day of holiday' feeling, it removes their head from the sand and switches on the light of crushing realization: 'Jesus wept, this is so much better than *my* everyday life. What the f**k am I doing?'

This contemporary angst is infiltrating our personal lives as well as our career and is tempting us, for instance, to jettison long-term relationships that are stable, but latterly might have lacked excitement or passion. This perspective now often crystallizes in middle age, with the energy-sapping focus of children removed from the marital equation, and the prospect of decades of safe dullness until inevitable death now in clear view. The number of people over 50 shedding long-term marriages is steadily increasing. According to government figures, the overall number of divorces in the UK fell between 1998 and 2000. But in the same period, divorces in the 50–59 age group rose by 8.7%, and those in the 60+ age group rose by 8.9%. Kate Vetrano, an American legal specialist on late divorce, confirms a similar picture in the United States: 'So many of this generation are sitting with the prospect of many happy, healthy years ahead of them. They're shedding their marriages in the quest for happiness.'

(Of course, the individual impatience that characterizes the modern age does often provoke warranted anxiety or criticism. Indeed, it is highly questionable whether upward trends in divorce rates, or the dumbing down of language or the media to cater for lower concentration spans, are positive social developments. But in the sphere of work, this restlessness is surely positive, preventing people from mindlessly following the path of unproductive boredom.)

Another sign that people are becoming increasingly restless with the reality of their lives is the rise of the life coach, who offers to help the individual gain focus, perspective and clarity on what is really important to them by asking questions, listening, and being an objective sounding board. In 1999, life coaching became the second fastest growing industry in the United States, after information technology. Karl Marx once wrote that 'the country that is more developed industrially only shows, to the less developed, the image of its own future'. What America, the leader of the capitalist world, does today, Britain does tomorrow. From about 500 trained life coaches in the UK in 2001, there are now thought to be well over 5,000, with thousands more queuing to join the mushrooming industry by obtaining qualifications of vastly varying quality from a myriad of coaching schools.

Tens of thousands of Britons have already invested in life coaching, principally from the ranks of white-collar workers. Millions more aspire to some coaching or professional counselling, but seem put off only by the cost (coaching is not cheap – an average 40-minute session costs around £80). A major study released by the British Association of Counselling and Psychotherapy in 2004 shows a marked shift in public attitudes towards therapy, once seen as a preserve for those with psychiatric or psychological problems. A remarkable 83% of Britons are now considering counselling. The BACP says its own membership has more than tripled in the last decade in order to meet the growing demand. The UK Council of Psychotherapy reports a similar rate of growth.

The self-help book market is the cheaper alternative to coaching or therapy, and offers solutions ranging from minor self-improvement to total life overhaul. In 1999, $588 million worth of self-help books were sold in America. In Britain, where sales are small by comparison, sales nevertheless almost doubled from £13.2 million in 1998 to £24.2m in 2000. And of course, it is logical to assume that now demand has been ignited, it will inevitably spiral. If one self-help book works, then the grateful reader will seek more in other areas of their life. In the overwhelming majority of cases where the self-help book is as effective as a plastic knife for a tree feller, the frustrated reader will scour the shelves for other sources of inspiration. As *The Economist* wrote in 2001: 'If you buy a book to fix a problem, and it works, you don't need another book. Fortunately for Britain's publishers, the sales graph in America (and the state of the American psyche) suggests that that is not a serious danger.'

જ

A further manifestation of the modern focus on meaning, fulfilment and the satisfaction of the inner self is the move away from traditional religion in favour of various forms of mysticism and spiritualism, such as reiki, t'ai chi, kabbalah, astrology and holistic healing.

In their book *The Spiritual Revolution: Why Religion is Giving Way to Spirituality*, Linda Woodhead and Paul Heelas, lecturers in religion at

Lancaster University, surveyed inhabitants of Kendal, Cumbria in order to chart the decline of Christianity and the corresponding rise in mysticism. During the 1990s, when the town's population grew by 11.4%, participation in the 'new spiritualism' grew by 300%, at the same time the church-going population, while still larger, fell considerably. Extrapolating this recent trend, the authors concluded: 'If the holistic milieu continues to grow at the same linear rate that it has since 1970 and if the congregational domain continues to decline at the same rate that it has during the same period, then the spiritual revolution would take place during the third decade of the third millennium.' That is, spiritualism will be more popular than Christianity thirty years from now.

Of course, followers of traditional religion would doubtless argue that their path offers more profound fulfilment than a yoga session a couple of times a week. But that is irrelevant to this discussion. What is significant is the trend away from the subjugation of the self for the purposes of the future greater good, towards a quest for the *immediate* satisfaction of the individual's singular and intrinsic needs. As Heelas explains: 'It's a shift away from (the idea) of a hierarchical, all-knowing institution and a move towards (having) the freedom to grow and develop as a unique person rather than going to church and being led. A lot of the comfort of religion is in postponement – a better life after death. But a belief in Heaven is collapsing, so people believe it is more important to know themselves and make themselves better people now.'

And how many people, after going through sessions with their life coach, or engaging in their spiritual soul-searching, are going to sit bolt upright, their wide-open eyes signalling that their long sought-after eureka moment has arrived, and then exclaim: 'Yes! Of course! Why has it taken me so long to work it out? It's so simple! I have to work in a massive office punching numbers into Excel spreadsheets, interspersed with long periods of doing absolutely nothing (apart from telling everyone else how busy I am).'?

The roots of unrest

Why the quest for fulfilment? Why such dissatisfaction, such lack of contentment? Maslow's hierarchy provides one answer. The materialism and quest for status, recognized as the defining characteristics of the 1980s, have not satisfied us but have simply elevated us to the next level, to the need for self-fulfilment and its accompanying uncomfortable and mysterious feeling of restlessness.

Another convincing explanation is that the greatly increased fluidity of the class structure in modern Western society supposedly makes success in working life attainable for all, and therefore makes failure to achieve that success more troublesome for the individual. Higher education, for instance, a necessary precondition to reaching the elite of most spheres of endeavour, is no longer the preserve of the tiny minority. This raises unrealistic expectations for many. The elites don't get any larger, and interesting and challenging jobs do not necessarily become more plentiful, just because more people can realistically aspire to them. Disappointment is thus inevitable, as Cary Cooper, professor of organizational behaviour at Lancaster Business School, explains: 'We have a problem at the moment with young professionals, and much of that is concerned with expectations of education ... The expectation is that if you get a degree you will get a great job. That isn't the case. Twenty years ago it was, but then only ten per cent of people went into higher education, and that figure is now over forty per cent ... People are getting fed up. They go through all the university exams and get a job, but find that it isn't as high-flying and exciting as they had imagined.'

When we were stuck in our class silos, our lives were largely determined by our social status, not our abilities. But now we don't have the same excuse. In a society perceived to be meritocratic, failure to scale the heights can damage confidence and cause introspection, as Alain de Botton points out in his book *Status Anxiety*: 'In a meritocratic world, where prestigious and well-paid jobs could be secured only on the basis of one's own intelligence and ability, it now seemed that wealth might be a sound sign of character. The rich were not only wealthier; they might also be plain better.' But for those at the bottom of the ladder, the reverse applies: 'If the successful merited their success, it necessarily followed that the failures merited their failure ... Low status came to seem not merely regrettable, but also *deserved*.'

The fact that we are still a long way off a pure meritocracy in the world of the large corporates is irrelevant. Perception is key. As discussed later in the book, the ambitious hopefuls further down the ladder want to believe that the Great Leaders are invested with near-divine qualities because it makes their own journey to the summit more meaningful and rewarding. They deny the reality of clannishness and patronage (although they tacitly accept them through their actions), preferring to attribute company success to ability and conscientiousness. Anyone who has worked in a large company will recognize the strangely reverential tones with which people often talk about their Great Leaders.

So if we buy into this idea of meritocracy (and in many fields outside of the large corporates, the idea will often have much more justification), it follows that failure to climb up the ladder hurts not just the pay packet but also an individual's view of himself. If we do try to ascribe lack of success to being excluded from the obligatory club or even just to plain bad luck, our behaviour is deemed churlish and unreasonable: 'Listen to him, he'll blame anyone and anything apart from himself.' So we take it on the chin and search desperately for short cuts to climbing the ladder, or for a wholly different sphere of activity that might be more suited to our talents, and thereby offers us recognition, status and the resulting self-respect. Alternatively, we just opt out of the system completely and very obviously switch our ambitions away from career and wealth. If we 'downshift', nobody can criticize us for failing because we have plainly rejected conventional, or money-oriented, definitions of success and failure. We might have made high status unattainable, but we have also rendered ourselves immune from the negative judgements of others and released ourselves from our own self-doubt.

This feeling of inadequacy and frustration is compounded by the proximity of success. We can almost reach out and touch it. The expansion of opportunity means that most of us personally know people who have really made it. And even if we don't, the media bombards us with stories of the lives of the rich and famous, and those who have escaped the humdrum, together with advice on how to improve our house, our finances and our abilities to attract the opposite sex. Thus, a self-reinforcing process is triggered. We are restless because society now seemingly offers us the real possibility of success, together with its bedfellow, the disconcerting spectre of failure, and we therefore want to improve or escape. The media, ever sensitive to the desires of the consumer, offer us images of escape and means for improvement, thus inflaming desires and exacerbating fears yet further.

☙

In this environment of greater social fluidity and opportunity, it is natural that the most restless will be the most talented. Openings that recognize and nurture their abilities must be out there somewhere – it's just a matter of finding them. If fiercer external competition, for reasons explained later, simply makes large companies even more political rather than more meritocratic, the talented are more likely to seek opportunities outside the corporate world. In boom years especially, many large companies might join the much-heralded 'war for talent', a phrase coined in 1998 by McKinsey, the management consultancy, to denote the growing phenomenon of aggressively seeking and recruiting able workers.

But even if large companies see a need for talent and throw money at the problem, they are still surely in the long run fighting a losing battle in a modern world where people feel that they want to 'make a difference' or really make it big. Can you do that when you have 50,000 colleagues in the same organization? As the original 'War for Talent' article points out: 'Small companies exert a powerful pull across the whole executive spectrum, offering opportunities for impact and wealth that few large firms can match.' Despite its novelty and extreme riskiness, the startup revolution of the late 1990s proved irresistible to many of the most able. 25% of Harvard's 1999 MBA class, about 225 students, joined companies with fewer than 50 employees, rather than the traditional destinations of banking and consulting.

A disproportionate number of the talented and restless are likely to be women. If ever you want an argument to show that large corporates are anything but meritocratic, just point to the number of women in senior positions. In 2003, only 9% of FTSE 100 board members were women. 32 of the 100 companies had no female directors at all. There was only one female CEO and one female chairman. In America, things were only slightly better, with 13.6% of board members in the top 500 companies being women and eight female CEOs.

Some gender disparity in senior representation might be inevitable given the crucial career years in which many women are rearing children, but the level of the disparity is so great that it can in no way be explained away simply by the family factor. Another major reason surely must be that obtaining the patronage required to climb the corporate ladder often requires a chummy (and therefore, usually, male) disposition. The level of frustration felt by many talented individuals working in a large corporate is thus magnified for women. While there might be only 13.6% female representation on large company boards in the US, 28% of entrepreneurs are women (i.e. women-owned businesses account for 28% of all privately-owned businesses). The recruitment company, Korn Ferry International, investigated the apparent trend of female middle managers leaving large companies in a study entitled *Why Women Executives Leave Corporate America for Entrepreneurial Ventures.* 78% of the women taking part in the study said the opportunity to take risks with new ideas and test personal limits were the chief reasons for trading their jobs with large companies for ones with smaller, entrepreneurial outfits. And this female trend is apparently gaining pace. In the UK, according to the Global Entrepreneurship Monitor, the gap between male and female startup companies narrowed by 40% in 2002.

Ethnic minorities are similarly excluded from that anti-competitive oligarchy, the club of large company senior management. A pitiful 1% of FTSE 100 board members are from ethnic minority backgrounds.

⊙

Robert Frost, the American poet, once said: 'The brain is a wonderful organ. It starts working the moment you get up in the morning and does not stop until you get into the office.' The tension between talent and the traditional workplace is only likely to grow. How long can a highly intelligent individual deceive himself that devising strategies to expand the market for Yorkie chocolate bars in Eastern Europe is a serious intellectual challenge? Intellectual effort is required for the self-delusion, not for the job. But in these days of introspection and honesty, self-delusion has a limited life span. Averil Leimon, director of the British coaching firm White Water Strategies, says that research among her firm's clients and human resource directors at large companies suggests there is 'a recurring theme of people who you would define as successful getting to a point where they are demotivated and unproductive. When you scratch the surface of this, you find that they're bored'.

Indeed, genuine intellectual ability (not necessarily academic prowess but a lively and curious mind) is required for only a limited number of jobs in a large company, positions that usually involve the vital task of shaping the strategic direction of the company. Talented people might be becoming more dissatisfied with large companies because they feel they cannot satisfy their own personal dreams when working for them. But large companies themselves are arguably misguided, anyway, when they seek out talented people for all but the most cerebral roles in the first place. As Lucy Kellaway wrote in the *Financial Times*: 'Think what characterizes the really intelligent person. They can think for themselves. They love abstract ideas. They can look dispassionately at the facts. Humbug is their enemy. Dissent comes easily to them, as does complexity. These are traits that are not only unnecessary for most business jobs, they are actually a handicap when it comes to rising through the ranks of large companies.'

Highbrow strategy consultancy companies thus fulfil two major functions. Their clients, risk-averse senior management teams, can point to impressive-sounding words from consultants supporting conclusions that they had often already come to independently, and 'let's face it, those egg-heads at McKinsey must be right, so let's go ahead'. Secondly, instead of their brain atrophying within a large company environment where there will always be far more people with potential than there are interesting or influential roles (and where anyway, as we shall see later, those interesting and influential jobs often go to the well-connected rather than the able), thousands of very clever people can earn a non-academic wage while pursuing intellectually challenging and varied research and project work in a consultancy.

An impressive talent pool lies stagnant alongside the ranks of the Living Dead. Not necessarily people with absolutely nothing to do, but those who could do their impressive-sounding jobs standing on their heads while listening to their personal stereo and playing on their Xbox, and who therefore qualify as sufferers from a condition known to psychologists as 'underload syndrome', a lack of stimulation at work. Martyn Dyer-Smith, a psychologist at the University of Northumbria and a specialist in this area, agrees that the highly-skilled are particularly vulnerable to the syndrome, 'because they have perfected their skills and are able to perform their jobs with little effort. The carrot of a good salary makes them continue, but actually they don't have enough to occupy them'. The effects of this boredom can be far-reaching. Dyer-Smith asserts that long-term boredom has the same impact on the body as stress, leading to heart trouble and suppression of the immune system.

Of course, people in the industrial era have always been bored in their jobs. *Bartleby the Scrivener*, which vividly depicts the sterility and joyless routine of life in a Wall Street law office, was written by Herman Melville as far back as 1853. Karl Marx also wrote at length about the alienation of men in a capitalist society. It is not the boredom that is new, it is the intolerance of it and the willingness to acknowledge it. The acceptability of dissatisfaction and open admission of boredom and frustration make restlessness contagious. Every individual standing up and saying that what they are doing for a job is (not to put too fine a point on it) bollocks, switches that light on again in the minds of others and hence triggers or exacerbates their restlessness. The 'mustn't grumble' generations are dying out, and the 'life is too short' generations are slowly taking their place.

Boredom and the corporate future

The bad news for the corporate world is that this entire process is only just beginning. Large companies will surely struggle to keep up with the demands of a workforce who are increasingly resistant to the dull routine of office life. (Of course, lone business people and those who work in a small office will also have to experience the daily grind. But even the dullest, most routine, task suddenly acquires appeal as soon as the individual feels a genuine personal stake in its successful completion. Indeed, the alienation discussed by Marx results from the emotional distance between the worker and the products of his labour: 'The object that labour produces, its product, stands opposed to it as something alien, as a power independent of the producer' (*Manuscripts*, 1844)).

Just look at the pace of the rise of expectation and individual ambition. A mere two generations ago, our grandparents were fighting a war against an aggressive and brutal foreign force intent on destroying our way of life. Many of their own fathers had sacrificed their lives on the battlefields of the First World War. We are only two generations past the resignation among young males that they would very probably soon have to down tools and go to fight in a bloody war. And look at us now, dreaming all day of jacking in our well-paid and cushy jobs in our safe and warm offices and going out in search of individual 'meaning' and 'fulfilment'. If, two generations in, we don't know we're born, what will be the attitude of those who literally haven't been – our grandchildren?

Downshifting, life coaching, the vocabulary of purpose and fulfilment, the replacement for many of traditional religion by spiritualism – these phenomena are all very new on the scene. Only twenty years ago, the preoccupation of the British nation centred on the miners' strike, a period which now seems to symbolize the death throes of our identification with collective concerns, and the termination of the belief that our own personal fate is bound up with the fortunes of the social class to which we belong.

The speed with which the individual has triumphed over the collective has traumatized a society that had previously identified so strongly with nation and class. A clear sign of this trauma is the strange, popular display of grief that follows high-profile deaths or murders of people totally unacquainted with the grieving, the so-called 'Diana factor'. Or the ubiquitous flags of St George, that have recently emerged whenever the England football team play in a major tournament. Conscript-fought wars and class struggles have disappeared with great suddenness, together with the collective purpose and spirit that they engendered. A bereft populace consequently seek out alternative events around which to cohere, however insubstantial they may seem. This may well be a transitional phase in the relentless process of individuation, the Nicorette to wean us off the cigarettes before we give up completely.

The corporate world has tried opportunistically to fill the vacuum by positioning itself as the new cohesive force. But, as the workplace surveys demonstrate, companies have failed to inculcate a sense of community or a genuine commitment to the cause which might provide the sought-after meaning in the lives of their employees. People might talk the language of the corporate 'family', but it is simply empty jargon employed as a signal to project an image of conformity, a necessary attribute for the ambitious in corporate life.

The silliness of describing in such terms 50,000 people from different countries and backgrounds who just happen to be employed by the same organization that sells insurance or plastic cups is surely obvious to all the sane-minded. (The chief executive of one company which had lost large numbers of employees in the September 11 terrorist attacks referred to the 'grief' felt by the company 'family': 'Rest assured that we will do everything in our power to look after our own as can be seen with outpouring from our people all over the world. Our family sticks together, because families support each other. Families never forget their members.' How can people forget others they never knew in the first place? Anyway, what about all the 'members' who had been made redundant in the past? You can't sack a real family member. This type of language is not only nonsense, but deeply insensitive to the real grief of real families.)

Indeed, far from employer loyalty producing corresponding commitment from the employee, it is surely the clear lack of such loyalty that is exacerbating restlessness in the workforce. The 'job for life' psychological contract of the post-war era has gone, so any worker's push for freedom meets with less resistance from the more conservative side of his nature or from his dependants. It is now not so much 'yes, it's boring, but I've got a regular wage and a young family and a pension', but more 'I could be out any minute, look what happened to my mate Steve, I need to control my own future. Those bastards don't give a toss about me, so f**k them, I'll look after number one'.

This, and other factors contributing to the rise of workplace restlessness, are themselves very much recent products of the modern era. They will not only not disappear, they will inevitably grow in significance and influence. Economic security, class fluidity, the expansion of higher education and individual opportunity, the rightful impatience of women and ethnic minorities, the climate of honest self-reflection, the disappearance of the 'job for life' – all these causes of unrest are in their infancy. The unrest will be accelerated by the media responding to popular demand for means of improvement and images of escape, and by the contagion of so many others expressing their disillusionment, and acting upon it.

So, having failed to elicit purpose and satisfaction through their false propaganda of corporate unity, how will companies treat the fast-spreading diseases of aimlessness, demotivation and ennui? The first step, as always, must be the ruthlessly honest recognition of the truth, uncloaked in jargon. It is now not just individual companies that have to work hard to prevent their staff from being poached by rivals. The entire corporate world will increasingly be forced to contend with growing dissatisfaction among its employees and the pull of alternative ways of living and working. This will be its key test in the coming generation, and how it responds will be fascinating to watch.

ꛯ

The next three chapters will examine the causes of Living Death and how companies can get ahead of the competition by stemming this tide of discontent. A revolution in people management, designed to combat individual listlessness and boredom will necessarily be high on their agenda. But however successful companies become in motivating employees, it is doubtful whether life in large organizations will remain sufficiently attractive to avert a significant exodus of those who seek to inject a more profound purpose into their lives. The incompatibility of corporate life and the modern world will be most keenly felt by the talented. The thousands who will be cast off by the corporate world because of the huge inefficiencies illuminated by intensifying competition will be joined by many more who refuse to while away the best years of their lives doing jobs that satisfy their bank manager, but not them.

William H. Whyte, in his 1950s classic *The Organization Man*, bemoaned the post-war triumph of corporate 'groupthink', suppression of creativity and the preoccupation with financial security over the core values of the American Dream, individualism and entrepreneurialism. He would be starting to feel much happier now. Submissiveness and low expectations are both sliding off the contemporary menu.

Life's a bitch, and then you leave your company.

ꛯ

CHAPTER 5

THE WHOLE TRUTH AND NOTHING BUT

'What bullshit essentially misrepresents is neither the state of affairs to which it refers nor the beliefs of the speaker concerning that state of affairs. Those are what lies misrepresent, by virtue of being false. Since bullshit need not be false, it differs from lies in its misrepresentational intent. The bullshitter may not deceive us, or even intend to do so, either about the facts or about what he takes the facts to be. What he does necessarily attempt to deceive us about is his enterprise. His only indispensably distinctive characteristic is that in a certain way he misrepresents what he is up to.'

From On Bullshit by Harry Frankfurt, Professor of Philosophy Emeritus at Princeton University

D ishonesty lies at the very core of the corporate system. Not brazen lying and stealing by employees, or alleged corporate exploitation of people and countries, as suggested by the Naomi Klein/ Michael Moore brigade. But the dominance of image over reality, of obfuscation over clarity, of politics over performance. As Corinne Maier said of life in a large organization, private or public: 'It's a make-believe world with make-believe language and make-believe jobs. All that the employee is asked to do is to make believe that they are working.'

There will of course be people within these organizations who work extremely hard. These might be individuals with rare but valuable expertise. They might have unusually transparent and measurable roles, such as a sales person or a professional whose services are charged out by the hour. They might be middle managers, bogged down in administration and budgets, who don't have the will or the scope to delegate work.

But no matter how hard you try, you just can't get away from these people. Open any newspaper, tune in to a radio phone-in or read one of the many books about stress and overwork published in recent years, and you will find out all you need to know about them. They are all ill, they are depressives, they are divorced, they are alcoholics, they've been signed off work by their doctor, they're so busy that they haven't seen their children since 1974, three years before they were born, they're too stressed to have sex and their genitals have disintegrated through under-use.

These people are undoubtedly a reality, although it is difficult to help feeling that their predicament and their prevalence are somewhat overplayed by our 'progressive' classes to make their own political point. Madeleine Bunting's *Willing Slaves – how the overwork culture is ruling our lives* is a fine example of this leftist preoccupation with long hours, overwork and stress. The 'ragged trousered philanthropists' of the Edwardian past might have swapped their tatty overalls for an Armani suit, so the story goes, but those evil capitalists are still demanding their pound of flesh. They just have to find ever more cunning ways to achieve their shameless ends.

Little allowance is made, in this narrative, for the reality that many are overworked simply because they are genuinely fulfilled by their jobs (or prefer them to their home lives) and genuinely enjoy working long hours because of this. Bunting argues: 'Life is work, work is life for the willing slaves who hand over such large chunks of themselves to their employer in return for the pay cheque ... The logical conclusion, unless challenged, is capitalism at its most inhuman – the commodification of human beings.' Anyway, you probably get the picture.

So let's talk for a change about the millions who are almost never given a mention, the people who do nothing or very little for long periods. And the dishonesty, which is such a dominant facet of corporate culture, is the main cause of this widespread inactivity in office life.

There are two principal types of perennially inactive employee. There are those who are content with their predicament, benefit from it, possibly even engineer it; and there are those who feel that their working lives are devoid of all meaning, and have stripped them of their energy and zest – the Living Dead. To differentiate the former from the Living Dead, I have given these particular actors in the corporate spectacle a separate label – the Professional Operator.

The Professional Operator manipulates the opacity of the system, plays politics, cultivates alliances and carefully manufactures his or her own image to climb up the ladder (or remain in their current position of strength) without the intrusive inconvenience of doing much work along the way. *The Office's* David Brent, or Lucy Kellaway's character Martin Lukes are classic caricatures of this hated, but very familiar, breed. (At least, that is, everyone *claims* they hate the dedicated political corporate animal, none more so than the political corporate animals themselves. 'I hate politics' is often the cry of those who seek to divert attention away from their own latest ruse. Telling all and sundry in the office that you hate politics is itself an obvious act of corporate politics. The label 'political' is a handicap to the corporate career, *being* political is a great help – one more example of workplace hypocrisy.)

The Living Dead, on the other hand, are often frustrated victims of the dishonesty that is built into the corporate system. They might lack the ability or the will to participate in political games. They might simply not be cut out for it, they feel ridiculous when they attempt falseness – it doesn't sit comfortably with them. They don't care sufficiently about achieving corporate success for them to acquiesce in subjugating their true personality in the pursuit of it. Instead, they opt out. They become gradually disillusioned and cynical, excluded from the mainstream, shunted to the periphery of company life. They lose hope, their spirit and any sense of what it once was which differentiated them as individuals from the remaining hordes of the Living Dead.

In the aftermath of the release of her book, *Bonjour Paresse*, Corinne Maier was hauled before the disciplinary board of her company, Electricité de France, for committing the worst possible sin in corporate life – exposing the truth about all of this. (Indeed, her book probably contained more reality and honesty than you will find in the entire Business section of your local Waterstone's – apart from *The 90-Minute Manager*, of course, which is a veritable classic.) She was accused of 'aiming to spread gangrene in the system from within' for saying things like 'you just have to show off and to make the others believe that you work very hard. And if you are really good in acting, you can make a very big career'. Or 'working for large corporations is like being in a giant washing machine, spinning around, going nowhere. Just go through the motions. You might even get promoted'. Talk about touching a raw nerve.

I would have found it difficult to write *The Living Dead* while still employed. I would doubtless have been hauled before my company's Great Leaders (who would have known deep down that what I am saying is completely true) to explain my 'negative' stance, despite the fact that my own story serves to expose the gross inefficiencies in their organizations and could be used as a spur to improve the system. This type of dishonest charade, or the totally rational self-censorship which so many workers sensibly employ, is standing full square in the way of progress. It is doing nothing less (and I'm choosing my words carefully here) than holding back the development of the capitalist world.

Firstly, as discussed above, because the basic dishonesty inherent in the corporate system causes millions of Professional Operators and Living Dead to be so unproductive, and that's not great for the old GDP. And secondly, because honest and open debate is in itself a mechanism for progress, and without it, such progress is impossible. As any alcoholic is told before his first meeting at Alcoholics Anonymous, you can't make progress unless you face the reality, no matter how unpleasant that reality is.

One of the central tenets of the Western system of liberal democratic capitalism is indeed free and open debate. Through the clear establishment of the facts exposed by the free press, free debate is entered into by a free intelligentsia and a free populace. The strengths and weaknesses of all arguments are explored in detail, weak ideas fall by the wayside, strong ideas stand the test of scrutiny, and a general consensus on how to move forward is reached. Mistakes will inevitably be made, but freedom allows those mistakes to be identified and hopefully rectified. Openness is thus the agent of human progress.

This chapter examines in further detail the causes and damaging consequences of dishonesty and of the lack of such openness within three separate areas of the business world – its literature, its language and its politics.

Business books – an expensive alternative to Andrex?

In August 2004, *The Economist* published an article debating the business book market, subtitled 'why so many business books are awful'. I read the article eagerly, hoping that it would help to explain this strange but fascinating phenomenon. Unfortunately for me, the article did not answer the question in its own sub-title, but did provide an accurate description of the dross served up by the business book market:

> 'Many appear to be little more than expanded PowerPoint presentations, with bullet points and sidebars setting out unrelated examples or unconnected thoughts. Some read like an extended paragraph from a consultant's report (and, indeed, many consultancies encourage their stars to write books around a single idea and lots of examples from the clientele). Few business books are written by a single author; lots require a whole support team of researchers. And all too many have meaningless diagrams.'

There is one theme running through this paragraph that provides one answer to the article's sub-title. As *The Economist* doesn't seem to want to say it outright, here goes: Laziness. Business authors just can't be bothered putting in the huge effort to write properly. They regurgitate previous presentations, bung them willy-nilly in the text without the thought required to identify the best position for them, they work with others to cut down the workload, and pad out their books with lots of pointless graphs and mind-numbing and inane anecdotes from other people. Cut and paste – the motto of the business author.

This laziness is also often manifested in business writers' excessive over-simplification, their avoidance of any challenging complexity, their obsessive reductionism. All manner of problems have a strangely finite solution. *The Economist's* ironic advice to the budding business author: 'Copy Stephen Covey (author of the hugely successful *Seven Habits of Highly Effective People*) and include a number. Here, though, inflation is setting in: this autumn sees the publication of *The 18 Immutable Laws of Corporate Reputation* by Ronald Alsop. And Michael Feiner has written a book offering 'the 50 basic laws that will make people want to perform better for you'.

Not 49, not 26, not 73, but 50. Here are a few other recent ones I found on a one-minute Internet search. *Don't Oil the Squeaky Wheel: And 19 Other Contrarian Ways to Improve Your Leadership Effectiveness* by Wolf Rinke; *Charisma: Seven Keys to Developing the Magnetism that Leads to Success* by Tony Allesandra; *Executive Charisma: Six Steps to Mastering the Art of Leadership* by D.A. Benton; *How to Think Like a CEO: The 22 Vital Traits you need to be the person at the top* by D.A. Benton; *How to Act Like a CEO: 10 Rules for Getting to the Top and Staying There* by D.A. Benton (this woman Benton sure is numerate – if her books ever flop she should apply for a job as The Count von Count on *Sesame Street*).

Why such laziness? In a piece from 2003, the novelist Andrew Crumey asked the question: 'Why if the captains of industry are so smart, are their books so awful?' He went on: 'Let me describe a typical example of the genre. The title includes a word like "win", "succeed" or "performance". Inside, there are lots and lots of bullet points. If there is one thing I know about business, it is the importance of the bullet point, and maybe a big box to emphasize that this is a Really Big Idea. Perhaps the need for such succinctness is proof of how genuinely busy the authors of these books are, with scarcely a moment to jot down a few inspirational ideas before leading their companies to ever greater heights.'

There is certainly something in this tongue-in-cheek explanation. Laziness masked as busyness is a common feature of the business world. Looking busy is proof of success, being unexpendable and irreplaceable. Being busy, however, is often too much like hard work. There are several people I have worked with who are congenitally lazy, but when they pick up their work phone, they say their name quickly and breathlessly like a heroic cop in an action movie telephoned by his partner on the way to capturing a dangerous murderer in the act. 'I'm picking up my phone despite the fact that I am extraordinarily busy which of course is because I am so indispensable.' From booking their holiday online to Jack Bauer in one ring of the phone. (While I'm on the subject, the fast and purposeful walk around the office is also generally used to create the false impression of busyness. Many times, looking at somebody racing across the office floor, I have had a bubble coming out of my head which said something like 'stop walking so fast, you prat, you haven't got anything to do'.)

This dishonest pace and rhythm of language is evident in every office and has also, as Crumey hints, pervaded the literature of business. The short sentences and bullet points give the impression of busyness elsewhere. 'I'm just taking a short interlude on the red-eye from LA between other pressing assignments to write these brief but pithy words for my next business book for the benefit of my incredibly busy readers' is the impression sought. The reality is Ctrl+V on your keyboard and waiting for one of your 17 co-authors to write something interesting, which they won't do because they can't be bothered either.

Another reason for the laziness is that the authors know full well that hardly anyone will actually read the content, so why bother? A business book is not there to be read, is it? The actual reading of the book is not part of the unwritten psychological contract between writer and buyer. This contract goes something like this: 'I'll rustle up a quick book, you buy it because it will make you feel or look better, and I'll then be able to sell myself more in the management seminar circuit, where I can make you or your company look or feel better.'

Corporate strategy books are bought to be placed unread on office shelves to give the impression of being up with the latest thinking. (There must be more readers than buyers of certain great books, as copies are passed around on recommendation. The ratio of bought versus read for the average business best-seller, on the other hand, must be about ten thousand to one.)

Self-help books are bought to make the buyer feel that he is doing something to improve his life, several aspects of which he is unhappy with for whatever reason. He will then skim-read to find any lessons he can apply as a quick fix. Meanwhile, the author is getting what he wants from the contract – not the satisfaction of writing a useful book but the promotion of his name, which he can then sell in countless management seminars which themselves are eagerly bought by companies seeking to be seen to be doing the right thing, or by individuals wanting to get ahead in their careers, and who think that listening to someone stating the obvious in business-speak for a couple of days might just do the trick. (Of course, all authors are interested in promoting their name, but only in the business book market does the motivation of potential future earnings through the promotion of the author's name seem so dominant.)

I came out with this opinion a while back to a professional management coach who was writing a book to add to the huge pile of coaching books already available on the shelves. 'A business book is almost always written purely to promote the author's name, and not in any way to say anything interesting, original or useful', I said, before smugly sitting back in my chair expecting an angry denial. Instead, I was made to feel like a naïve idiot devoid of any street-wise business acumen who was saying something blindingly obvious. 'Of course', the aspiring author replied, a knowing smile on his face aiming to advertise his astuteness.

You never know as well, you might actually hit the jackpot and write a book with a snappy title that catches a mood and begins to sell well. (Business publishers play the percentage game by releasing thousands of books in the knowledge that some of the dross, by the law of averages, will sell well and compensate for the majority which don't.) As the business book buyer is often solely interested in appearances, the 'tipping point' at which the book simply has to be bought by anyone who wants to be taken seriously actually arrives quite soon, after which sales no doubt accelerate at breakneck speed as thousands feel obliged to jump on the bandwagon.

As for the self-help genre; well, if so many others are buying a book which offers to turn the reader into a charismatic leader who earns pots of cash and bags plenty of decent-looking chicks along the way, then you'd better buy it, or you might end up a poor and uninteresting virgin, while everyone else is getting on board their private jet to service their adoring band of groupies.

⁓

Going back to *The Economist*'s sub-title of 'Why so many business books are awful', I would offer another contribution to the explanation. Just as there is a disincentive for the individual worker within the corporate world to express honest criticism, so there is a similar disincentive for the business author. Whereas the biographer or the historian might be lauded for taking a contrary and original view, if expressed intelligently and convincingly, the business author perceives little gain from challenging, or even honestly describing, the status quo. As discussed in Chapter 1, the Esteemed Guru writes his book to obtain lucrative work from corporates. He is not going to get that if he tells them that their working practices are hopelessly inefficient, that most of their workforce will never give a damn about an organization so large and impersonal, that many of them do pretty much nothing every day, and that their Great Leaders are only where they are because, early on in their careers, they selected the right arses to crawl up. As very few read what you write anyway, the best strategy is to jot down a few gentle but pretty superficial and meaningless observations and attach a sellable and memorable phrase to them. Never write too much that is negative or critical. God knows, too much of the truth and you never know what might happen – we might even be able to improve the way we work.

Alternatively, you can write a self-help book that accepts without any hint of criticism the premise that image is more important than performance in the workplace. Thus you can aim to teach the reader the hidden formula for individual corporate success, or how to hone their interview 'technique', or how to play the hugely destructive game of office politics, itself, as will be discussed later, a symptom of dysfunctional working practice.

It's enough to make you weep.

What the hell are you on about?

The lack of vigorous, clear and honest debate in business literature is retarding progress. The business-speak or jargon which so many individuals use in an office situation is itself proof that much progress needs to be made.

Why do people use business-speak when they are at work? Lucy Kellaway, columnist and long-time chronicler of business jargon, identifies seven reasons: 'habit; because it is deliberately vague; because it is a euphemism; because the jargon word is sometimes the only one that does the job; because it is easier to talk jargon than to say what you mean; because it sounds impressive; and because it makes you sound as if you are a member of a club.'

Euphemism is generally used by an employer or a government seeking to soften bad news, such as the internal memo, quoted by Kellaway, of a company informing its staff that there would be no imminent pay rises: 'Once we attain our stretch performance goal with consistent momentum going forward, we will reopen our salary review process for all non-commissioned employees and make additional adjustments at that time.'

Unfortunately, those in authority will frequently have to impart bad news, and inevitably it is their natural tendency to attempt to soften the blow, however ludicrous their attempts often appear. What is particularly interesting is why people lower down in an organization talk such bollocks – not write bollocks on an official memo, but *talk* bollocks to each other on an everyday basis.

Kellaway lists several verbs that have crept into office usage: 'to drive', 'to buy into something', 'to own', 'to grow' (as a transitive verb, as in 'to grow the bottom line'), 'to deliver', 'to leverage', 'to harness', 'to unveil', 'to task', 'to head up' (instead of 'to lead' – very annoying). Several phrases irritated me particularly: the ubiquitous 'going forward', to 'roll out', 'throw a curve ball', 'give someone a head's up'. Or seemingly innocuous phrases which are just annoying because people only use them when they are at work. One phrase that used to send me into a complete frenzy for some reason was 'I don't disagree with that'. Why do people say 'I don't disagree with that' in a workplace? Look you arse, does that mean you agree with it, or that you don't? If you agree, say you agree with it. If you agree with it only partially, state what your reservations are. Don't sit there desperately trying to create the image of a mature, statesmanlike businessman by saying 'I don't disagree with that' when nobody has a clue what you mean (not that anyone cares what you mean – this is the workplace after all).

Of all Kellaway's reasons for using jargon, the last one really rings true: 'because it makes you sound as if you are a member of a club'. Clearly this is true of industry-specific jargon, which dresses simple concepts in language that seeks to intimidate outsiders, lest they try to ask too many meddling questions or even attempt to enter the industry themselves, thus ratcheting up the competition for available jobs. But it is also true of more general business-speak. When somebody says during a meeting 'this is where we are, going forward' and everyone nods, the whole process has nothing to do with communicating and understanding a point. The speaker is not conveying information or an opinion – the sentence is clearly nonsense. The business-speak is a signal of loyalty, a demonstration that the speaker will play the corporate game without complaint, that he will never speak totally honestly, he will respect the right people in the hierarchy and will never rock the boat.

People might not speak grammatically, beautifully or with watertight logic outside work, but they talk normally and clearly enough to get their point across successfully. The use of jargon in the workplace is not, therefore, a result of people's inability to speak clearly. It is employed deliberately as a code that indicates conformity. In this way, business-speak has much in common with the jargon-filled language used in another environment where conformity was demanded, where honesty and clear thought merely inflicted damage on the speaker. Namely, the totalitarian environment of Nazism and Communism.

This might appear over-dramatic and insensitive – the scale of the punishment for rejecting conformity in the corporate world obviously does not bear comparison in any way with the horrors meted out in a totalitarian system. But even if the stakes are infinitely lower, the main reason for using the jargon is the same. Commentators routinely describe business-speak as Orwellian, as it was George Orwell who conceived Newspeak, the language of the totalitarian society envisaged in his book *1984*. Orwell divides Newspeak into three categories, one of which, the B vocabulary, is, according to the author, 'deliberately constructed for political purposes: words, that is to say, which not only had in every case a political implication, but were intended to impose a desirable mental attitude upon the person using them'.

Business jargon is clearly not deliberately constructed by cunning corporations seeking to own and control our minds. But the principal reason why people speak this very particular language of the workplace is indeed because it demonstrates 'the desirable mental attitude'. It serves as an advertisement to potential Powerful Patrons in the higher reaches of the organization: 'I'll toe the line. Please look after me.'

There is one further reason for using jargon that can be added to Kellaway's list. And the reason is this: 'because you can get away with it'. If you worked for a very small company in a competitive environment, you would not use business-speak, at least internally within the company. It would be absolutely essential that your colleagues understand you as clearly and as quickly as possible, because there would be no time to waste and mistakes would be highly damaging. There would be no point posturing, or desperately trying to be impressive. A very small company is too transparent – everyone knows what you are really up to every day, what your value to the business is. The fact that business-speak has entered the everyday language of discourse in larger offices is itself evidence that people instinctively realize that nobody really knows what anyone else is doing, and that image is therefore crucial. It's no wonder that in this environment, so many do nothing.

We will know when we are making progress towards transparency and meritocracy, and therefore towards efficiency and hard work, when every large office is resounding with the words, 'I'm sorry, what you have just said is utter gibberish – what on God's earth do you mean?'

Political murder

There are many books on the market that offer the reader advice on how to play or to endure the game of office politics, some serious and some humorous. It's no wonder there are so many. Politics is a huge economic problem for business. US executives say they waste 19% of their time – at least one day per week – dealing with company politics, according to a survey of 150 executives of major US firms by OfficeTeam, a California-based recruitment company. The executives surveyed said they spent much of that time dealing with internal conflicts, rivalry disputes and other volatile situations at work.

Britain is no different. According to a 2002 survey by Internet job site reed.co.uk of 1600 temporary workers, objective observers with no axe to grind and with experience of many different industries, the average workplace loses more than an hour's productivity every day through time-consuming office politics, with an estimated cost to business of £7.8 billion. Power struggles are cited as the most frequent cause of office politics by more than 40% of the respondents, followed by differences of opinion and favouritism.

Office politics, the practice of workplace dishonesty, occurs for exactly the same reason as jargon, the language of workplace dishonesty. And that is the absence of a transparent meritocracy. The essence of this logic is as follows: the huge machine of many large corporates will naturally produce business, using its global presence and brand name, however inefficient its people and processes. This inevitable revenue is then fought over by the employees of the company. Without a completely clear and transparent measurement system, an ambitious individual focuses on jockeying for position to appear as if he or she is closely associated to the revenue, not necessarily by being productive. The corporate does not generally require creativity or originality, as the business is already coming through the door, and little insight or talent is required by any one individual in order to process the business.

Political manoeuvring and patronage, not ability or productivity, are the engines of individual progress, hence the constant advertising of loyalty and conformity by the use of business-speak and other methods. You don't get politics in a very small company and you don't get it on a sports field. There is no point – your performance is there for everyone to see.

Many people do not have the inclination or the innate personality for this system of operating (possible candidates for a Living Death). Many of those that do will concentrate on self-publicity and forming strategic alliances rather than work (the Professional Operator). Inactivity is the inevitable result.

Those who do not involve themselves in this political battleground will inevitably comprise a disproportionate number of those with the most potential. Colin Gautrey, managing director of Politics at Work, a website that teaches people how to deal with office politics, says that a 'lot of very talented people are choosing to opt out of big companies because they are sick of the game-playing, which is a loss to industry'. In the last chapter, two reasons were suggested for the incompatibility, growing in the modern world, of large companies and people with ability and imagination. They were: the absence of opportunities to make a significant impact; and the small proportion of stimulating roles. The lack of transparency that in turn hinders the development of meritocracy is a third reason.

The most able clearly have the most to gain from meritocracy, and the least able have the most to gain from its absence. The ambitious and talentless will devote their lives to brown-nosing, backstabbing and seeking their own Powerful Patron. Employing this strategy is pretty much the only way they can succeed in life. Those with ability and ambition will naturally crave an environment in which they can seek the rewarding fulfilment of their potential and be recognized for it. The lucky ones manage either to find a suitable niche in their own companies, or to get out. Those less fortunate, or those with less drive to change their circumstances, or those trapped for financial or personal reasons, slump into cynicism and despondency, a Living Death, their talents wasted and long forgotten.

And internal politics, by all accounts, is getting worse, at least according to those at the grass roots of companies. In another survey developed by OfficeTeam, 720 employees and 150 executives from a selection of the United States' largest companies were asked the question: 'In your opinion, has the level of office politics increased or decreased compared with five years ago?' 36% of those lower down the organization replied that politics had 'increased greatly' and 34% said that it had 'increased somewhat'. But only 12% of executives interviewed said that it had 'increased greatly' and 29% said that it had 'increased somewhat'.

And it will no doubt get much worse, certainly for those at the bottom. Think of office politics as a game of musical chairs, the chairs being proximity to revenue or to those with invulnerable authority and influence within the organization, the Powerful Patrons and Great Leaders. The reason why fewer executives than employees believe that politics is getting worse is because many of them are already sitting comfortably in those chairs, oblivious and detached as usual and awaiting their next bonus, or maybe if they are lucky, a golden handshake followed by another golden hello. In their own personal lives, politics *has* subsided. As globalization takes greater hold, and external competition bites further into the revenue, fewer and fewer chairs will be available for those down below and the punishment for not sitting down will become more serious, as companies seek to cut costs. Unless companies change the way they operate, the political fight for those chairs will gradually become more brutal. This should not be regarded as healthy competition. Nobody is actually doing any work during this process.

e/o

Stress in the workplace is possibly often misunderstood. Many associate stress necessarily with overwork. My own personal suspicion is that the prevalence of overwork is exaggerated (working long hours and working hard are two different things – long hours themselves often result from image creation and politics, as we shall see in Chapter 7) and many who do work hard actually enjoy it. After all, enjoying one's job makes it possible to work hard. How many of us have the discipline to work hard, day in, day out, at something we don't enjoy? Stress and demoralization result more from other factors, and unpleasant office infighting features prominently among them.

In a 2003 study by the Irish Economic and Social Institute Survey, workers were asked to cite the main cause of their stress. 'Office politics' won hands down with 41%, with 'long working hours' way back at 18%. 'Difficult colleagues' came in at 17%, and as this by rights should fall within the 'office politics' category, we are left with a pretty good idea of what principally causes stress. In short, it results from being caught on the horns of a terrible dilemma – having to kowtow to people at work whom you despise or have no respect for, when such deference in the wider world has long since disappeared, in order to support yourself and the people you love.

The resulting stress inevitably saps morale and hurts productivity, all while the Great Leaders are upstairs sitting comfortably in their musical chairs. NFI Research, a US-based research company, quoted a respondent from their own survey into office politics: 'Senior management fosters the negative by turning a convenient blind eye and deaf ear. The impact of their inability to deal with the office politics is low morale, slower paces of work produced and encouraging employees not to care. Senior managers don't have the ability to deal with this escalating problem, so they ignore it.' You might add that most of them also don't care too much, for the time being anyway. They're all right, Jack.

External competition, which demands increased efficiency in response, is first and foremost causing an escalation of office politics, which in turn is actually reducing efficiency by supplementing the legions of the Living Dead. And, as already discussed, many of the disillusioned will have the most to offer. This indeed is the ultimate irony. As the climate of competition becomes more intense, companies will need employees of genuine ability at the top of the company, more than ever before, to help them to develop new strategies and methods of operating. But the principal consequence of this climate currently seems to be the augmentation of the worst effects of corporate life, alienating the very people companies will need in the future to lead them.

Clearly, if those with the most ability seek opportunities elsewhere, large companies will be left with the rump of the mediocre and the unimaginative. As Nigel Nicholson, a professor of organizational behaviour at London Business School, said: 'There is a global dearth of people who really have what it takes to be significant agents of change. The trouble is, that corporate culture kills off these people before they can climb the ladder. It's usually the safe people who manage to get to the top.'

A changing environment is coming up against a corporate world that is not reacting quickly enough, producing a negative impact on the motivation of its workers. It is not the modern world that is causing the stress, it is the fact that companies are reacting too slowly to the modern world.

But what, within large organizations, will precipitate transparency and meritocracy, the harbingers of efficiency and a constructive employee motivation, and the scourges of that great enemy of talent, workplace dishonesty? The answer, of course, is that large companies will have no option but to change (real change, not the 'change' beloved of our Great Leaders which either just makes people cynical or sends them to sleep). They will eventually be forced by the pressures of competition to undertake radical reforms, or face inevitable death. The speed and imagination with which they undertake these reforms will decide their ability to thrive in the real capitalist environment of the future – fluid, innovative, creative, dynamic, efficient, productive – the exact opposite of what so many of these corporate giants currently are.

The efforts, ideas and enterprise of many, including writers from a revitalized and revamped business book market, will be called upon during this period of change. And a necessary first step in this transformation is to begin to apply the same open, clear and honest scrutiny to the grim reality of corporate life and its causes that we apply to all other walks of life. Before progress, truth.

After truth, managers.

ల

CHAPTER 6

THE INVISIBLE MANAGER

'All great successes, all great lives have involved the coincidence of aptitude, talent but also the luck of meeting people who have believed in you. At some point in your life, you need someone who will tap you on your shoulder and say, "I believe in you".'

Arsène Wenger, Manager, Arsenal Football Club

W hen you're next with a group of friends, and the conversation is becoming a little monotonous, try this little experiment. Ask each of them to shout at the top of their voice if they have ever worked for a manager who wasn't absolutely appalling. Then just sit back and enjoy the blissful peace and quiet. Maybe enjoy a puff or two of your favourite cigar. Hum a little of Beethoven's Fifth.

Poor and absent middle managers are the abusive parents of the Living Dead. Without them, the Living Dead would not be created in the first place and certainly would not remain trapped indefinitely in their pointless existence.

We have become obsessed in these last celebrity-obsessed years with the cult of 'leadership', with the lone figurehead at the top of the organization. But our Great Leaders are irrelevant to the vast majority of workers in a large organization, although they would of course be horrified to learn *that* naked truth in the remote sanctuary of their corporate HQ. And here's another truth they won't like. Being a leader of your common-or-garden large company is generally very easy. At least, it is at present. You get paid loads, everyone looks like they are having the best sex of their life every time you open your mouth, and you can indulge every middle-aged man's fantasy of listening constantly to the sound of your own voice by pontificating ad infinitum about the future of your industry or your own company strategy. You either retire a demi-god, or get sacked, receive a huge pay-off and take the gravy train to your next destination, where yet more sycophants shake their heads in sheer disbelief at your incisive brilliance.

There are certainly quite a few people out there who could give that leadership lark a bash. Could they all manage a team of people so that they fulfil every last drop of their individual and collective potential? Not in a million years. Only a tiny few can do that.

The middle manager – the Viagra of the corporate world

Any honest assessment of the current state of business management makes for depressing reading. According to the Gallup Organization's Employee Engagement Index survey from 2003, 80% of British workers lack any real commitment to their jobs, and most blame poor management for their low level of motivation. As mentioned in Chapter 3, 20% are 'actively disengaged', or utterly disenchanted with their workplaces. Workers say they don't know what is expected of them, their managers don't care about them as people, their jobs aren't a good fit for their talents, and their views count for little. When workers talk of 'management', they will not be talking about their own line manager, not the chief executive or the board. It is a fair bet that most employees of a large company will not even know the name of their chief executive.

In another survey from 2003 entitled 'UK Line Managers – Are They Good Enough', the magazine *Personnel Today* reported that a paltry and measly 2% of UK human resources professionals interviewed stated that the people management skills of line managers in their companies were 'excellent', and 74% blamed ineffective line managers for low morale in their organization.

Indeed, the consequences of poor management are well documented. Research released in 1999 of Gallup interviews with more than a million employees in a broad range of industries, concluded as follows: 'Talented employees need great managers. The talented employee may join a company because of its charismatic leaders, its generous benefits and its world-class training programmes … but how long that employee stays and how productive he is while he is there is determined by his relationship with his immediate supervisor.'

The *Academy of Management Journal* conducted extensive analysis of the key motivating factors for a worker in an organization. Their conclusion was as follows: 'Although we found that overall commitment to organizations was uncorrelated with performance, we also found … that overall commitment to supervisors was positively and significantly associated with performance. Further … commitment to supervisors was more strongly linked to performance than was commitment to organizations.' ('Foci and bases of employee commitment: Implications for job performance, April 1996'.) And this is also, surely, the conclusion that any sane individual using basic common sense would arrive at. Does anyone seriously imagine that people leap out of bed in the morning just because they want to do their bit for the Shell or Unilever brand?

Small and very young companies might have a distinct atmosphere and ethos that inspire loyalty and commitment. But can a mature company, with tens of thousands of employees with very different personalities, using a variety of languages in more than 100 very different countries have a uniform 'culture'? The fact that so many leaders and gurus maintain that these cultures do exist is surely a result of either dishonesty or gross detachment from reality. There might possibly be a style or method of operating in the head office boardroom, but is this working culture disseminated into back offices in Kazakhstan and Bolivia, or even downstairs where the workers are?

The significance of the immediate supervisor is yet further borne out by a McKinsey survey published in 2000. Of 6500 senior and middle managers interviewed at 35 large companies in the United States, 58% said that they themselves worked for an 'underperforming manager'. Of those, 86% said that working for an 'underperformer' made them want to leave the company. The University of Michigan found that 80% of employees view their organization and their supervisor in exactly the same way. Manager great, company great. Manager terrible, company terrible. That is, even if a company's chosen corporate strategy is exciting, ground-breaking and awe-inspiring, even if the pay and perks are second-to-none, the workers will still be thoroughly unenamoured with the organization if they simply don't like their own manager. Similar surveys abound.

The financial repercussions of the widespread phenomenon of poor people management are considerable. The WorkUSA survey of 2000 found that companies whose workers are highly committed to their employers and have confidence in their management deliver dramatically higher returns to shareholders (a three-year return of 112% vs. 76% for committed vs. non-committed employees, and 108% vs. 66% for employees with high trust/confidence vs. low trust/confidence). The 2003 Gallup workforce survey estimates that actively disengaged workers cost the British economy between £37.2 billion and £38.9 billion due to absenteeism, poor performance and high employee turnover.

Another McKinsey survey, from 2002, revealed a clear relationship between good management and productivity, this time in the manufacturing sector. The survey assessed the value of three different facets of management: 'lean manufacturing' which minimizes waste; 'talent management', which attracts and retains high-calibre people; and 'performance management', which rewards employees who meet set goals.

To assess and measure the impact of these management techniques, McKinsey interviewed the directors of operations or of manufacturing at 100 companies in France, Germany, Britain and the United States. The companies were awarded a score for the standard of each management technique – the scores ranged from one (technique not being used at all) to five (reflecting 'best practice'). The company's score over a period of five years was then compared with several key financial indicators, the most important being the return on capital employed (ROCE) relative to the sector. The link between a company's management practices and its financial performance was significant. A one-point improvement in performance across all three management techniques, for example, generated a 5.1% increase in ROCE for companies. Over the five-year period, this improvement would equal the creation of a massive $400 billion in value for the US manufacturing sector, or a total of $700 billion for all four countries in the sample. 'To boost their ... productivity', McKinsey concluded, 'manufacturing companies are now inclined to lobby for tax breaks on capital investments, but our study shows that the same goals could be achieved, at little or no cost to governments or the sector, if managers managed better.'

Two clear facts have emerged here. Fact number one – management directly affects company performance and profitability. Fact number two – despite fact number one, management standards are pitifully low.

ℰℛ

So what can be done about all this? We need nothing less than a fundamental revaluation of the way in which middle managers are selected in large organizations, and a similar reassessment of how they would most profitably be deployed once ensconced in their position. We need to give a great deal more thought to what constitutes a good manager and then work much harder to seek out those who have what it takes to be that phenomenally rare breed – a manager who can inspire, cajole and encourage others to realize their potential. We then need to elevate the status, and the pay, of the able people manager. They are like gold dust to an organization. And as with everything in the business world, this whole exercise must be conducted in unambiguous and standard, everyday language which everyone can genuinely understand and therefore respond to and act upon. Anyone who uses phrases such as 'core competencies of leadership' is more interested in sounding impressive or being part of an exclusive club than in improving profitability.

But first, we need to take our Great Leaders aside, assure them that their ideas are of course fascinating and almost unbearably penetrating, we all had a little accident in the trousers department when they were giving their last presentation on strategy 'going forward', but quite frankly, all of it is just so much hot air unless they hire the right middle managers to communicate the thinking of the Great Leader, Blessed be He, and resuscitate the workforce from a state of boredom, cynicism and in many cases, outright Living Death.

The Great Leader is dead

Those at the summit of a large organization can swell the ranks of the Living Dead in two ways. Firstly, many of them might find delegation difficult, retaining virtually all decision-making powers for themselves. This might make them personally extremely busy, but will reduce the motivation of a neutered workforce who feel no ultimate responsibility for their work, and therefore no emotional connection to it. Secondly, their inevitable remoteness from the shop floor makes them oblivious to its bleak reality, and their resulting inaction allows disenchantment to consolidate and grow.

The thing is, deep down, the more discerning of our Great Leaders know the truth. How can they possibly even know what is going on in their mammoth organizations, let alone have much direct influence? Most of them, if they were honest, would probably admit that they don't know what's going on with their own families after being in the office for 80 hours each week.

In their book *The Hidden Power of Social Networks: Understanding how work really gets done in organizations,* Rob Cross and Andrew Parker quote an executive vice president in a commercial lending company. His candid admission of the inevitably limited influence of those high up in a large organization is particularly illuminating:

'Most of us in this room have thousands of people we are accountable for stretched across the globe. It's impossible to manage or even know what's going on in the depths of the organization. I mean, each of us can fool ourselves into thinking we're smart and running a tight ship. But really, the best we can do is create a context and hope that things emerge in a positive way, and this is tough because you can't really see the impact your decisions have on people. So you just kind of hope what you want to happen is happening and then sound confident when telling others.'

And confidence is not something our Great Leaders are normally short of, so the myth that the abilities of the higher echelons are principally responsible for large company performance lives on, to the detriment of the area that really counts, middle management.

Cross and Parker themselves hint at the futility of attempting to exert control over a large organization from on high. In reality, top executives will often not have the faintest inkling about what is actually happening at the grass roots: 'Reflect for a moment on the network of relationships among the people you work with. You can probably describe your close relationships accurately, but studies show that as you move beyond your immediate circle, your accuracy likely begins to fall off.'

Writing in the *Financial Times* in 2004, Stefan Stern highlights two high-profile examples of chronic senior management detachment. First, the collapse of Marconi in 2001: 'Even as senior managers were reassuring investors that order books were healthy, lower down the corporate hierarchy the awful truth was already apparent to the rest of the staff.' Second, the September 11th terrorist attacks: 'Central Intelligence Agency and Federal Bureau of Investigations operatives attempted to voice their concerns, in particular about the influx of young Saudis who were suddenly keen to learn how to fly. But their warnings never got through.'

Of course they didn't get through. Senior executives were no doubt preening themselves in front of the mirror at the time, after reading the latest fawning drivel about the enigmatic secrets of Great Leadership, as displayed by some of our foremost kings of the corporate world. Mountains of literature have been written about our Great Leaders by our Esteemed

Gurus in recent years as part of their mutually beneficial love-in, and much more by the Great Leaders themselves. It's amazing they have a few spare minutes to be such Great Leaders, the amount of time they spend boring us into submission talking or being interviewed about their remarkable journey to the summit of the corporate Mount Everest, propelled by their 'winning mentality' and their 'highly developed emotional intelligence'.

The January 2004 edition of the *Harvard Business Review* provides an excellent example of this insane and self-serving cult of Leadership. An entire issue was devoted to the subject. Firstly 18 'leaders and scholars' lined up to give us their earth-shattering tips on effective leadership. Get these for insightful nuggets of analysis: 'Never stop Learning'; 'Get Motivated'; 'Seek Frank Feedback'; 'Watch your Culture'; 'Sniff out Signals'; 'Keep it Honest'. It's hardly a wonder these guys get paid so much. The whole edifice of the market economy would crumble without their burning originality.

Next comes super-guru Warren Bennis, *distinguished* professor of business at the University of Southern California and author of *On Becoming a Leader*. He chronicles the life of a Great Leader through Shakespeare's seven ages of man, as follows: 'The Infant Executive'; 'The Schoolboy, with Shining Face'; 'The Lover, with a Woeful Ballad'; 'The Bearded Soldier'; 'The General, Full of Wise Saws'; 'The Statesman, with Spectacles on Nose (no doubt these are the annoying idiots who go around saying "I don't disagree with that" all day); and, finally, 'The Sage, Second Childishness'. At this final stage, the 'sage' becomes a teacher and mentor to others. Bennis urges the Great Leaders to seek solace in their awesome contribution to posterity as their frighteningly productive working life comes to a sad but inevitable end: 'When you mentor, you know that what you have achieved will not be lost, that you are leaving a professional legacy for future generations'.

I may not be a distinguished professor, but I have been inspired by these beautiful and thoughtful words to compose a humble stab at the seven ages of a Great Leader, based on my own, admittedly more shallow and limited, experience of the corporate world: 'The Normal Worker'; 'The Team Player'; 'The Observer of the Corporate Game'; 'The Arse-Licker'; 'The Shit Manager, with Bored Team'; 'The Licker of Important and Influential Arses'; 'The Out-of-Touch Leader, with Wads of Cash'. How much do I get for that, HBR?

Here's another classic from the Bennis stable. When asked for his recommendations for books on leadership, he replied: 'Read *Henry IV*, parts one and two, for a vision of heroic leadership. Glendower says, "I can call spirits from the vasty deep." And Hotspur replies, "So can any man; but will they come when you do call for them?" Courage is getting people to march behind your ideas. And read *Coriolanus*. He couldn't rise to the occasion when the situation was thrust on him.'

Poor old Coriolanus, he just can't hack it up there with Henry IV and the Great Leaders of the corporate world. Indeed, our Great Leaders are so all-knowing and wise that it is becoming increasingly difficult for them to find a role model from whom they *can* learn. Luckily, God is on hand to answer their prayers. Larry Julian's book *God is my CEO* looks at the earthly lessons which some of our more religious CEOs have gleaned from that Great Leader in the sky. Maybe this can be the start of a profitable two-way process. It's only a matter of time before some of our most awe-inspiring CEOs get invited inside those pearly gates so they can repay the debt and teach the Almighty a thing or two about running the Universe. I can just see a new opportunity for management conference organizers: 'Leadership – the way it's done down there'; Venue: The Heaven Hilton; Confirmed Speakers: Jack Welch and Stephen Covey; Who Should Attend: Saints, Future Messiahs, Guardian Angels, Seraphs. Price: £2435 plus VAT for 3 days, including gala dinners.

I'm sorry about all this but I've got some disappointing news for you, Mr. CEO of Joe Shmo plc or Mr. Head of Huge Department at Enormous Corporate Bollocks plc. Winston Churchill was a great leader. He inspired the British nation to fight with all its might to preserve our values of freedom and democracy against tyranny. That is leadership. Call me old-fashioned, but you are a run-of-the-mill company man who played a canny political game and got a few breaks. Nothing wrong with that, but let's not get carried away with ourselves, shall we?

Long live the manager

Where are we going wrong with management? The principal answer is that influential individuals in large organizations are not, in reality, personally motivated enough to get it right, to ensure that the grass roots are managed well, despite their predictable rhetoric and their going through the motions by investing in management training. A number of factors explain this.

One is what could be called the Self-Delusion of Corporate Success. When someone achieves high office, there is a natural self-aggrandizing tendency to attribute all that success to their own abilities and work ethic. This explains to some extent the willingness of the Great Leaders to participate in the cult of Leadership. It reaffirms their belief in their own unique abilities and provides a welcome explanation of why they are where they are in life. It also explains why ambitious people further down the company ladder are so in thrall of their leaders. It is not just sycophancy. They want to persuade themselves that every future step up the ladder is simply vindication of their own abilities and hard work. If they get to the top, where they long to be, it will be because of their talent and conscientiousness and nothing else. This gives them the necessary purpose and positive self-image as they strive to ascend the corporate hierarchy.

Clearly, in some environments, such as professional sport, a meritocracy does indeed exist. If you are exceptionally talented and you work hard, you will get to the top. Performance is totally transparent and counts for everything. Sycophancy might make your manager like you, but it won't get you in the team. Personal alliances and networking with other players might make you popular in the dressing room, but again, they won't get you in the team.

Some business environments and some companies, notably the smaller ones, are more meritocratic than others. But in a large corporate body, aspiring individuals require assistance at crucial stages of their career from two types of individual. Early on in their company life, they need a manager who plays to their strengths, encourages them, pushes them to the next level and in general provides what the management author Charles Handy describes as 'the golden seed', the spark of confidence and self-belief which every successful individual requires. If people, on the other hand, are neglected early in their careers, it will not be long before the poison of cynicism and bitterness sets in, and that is difficult to eradicate.

A little later in their career, the corporate hopeful also needs a Powerful Patron, who will look after their interests as part of an unspoken political pact. You make me look good, talk about how great I am to everyone down there and I will make sure you are promoted. The more meritocratic the environment, the more transparent an individual's real contribution to the business itself, the less important the Powerful Patron becomes.

But neither the manager nor the Powerful Patron feature prominently in the senior person's own retrospective career autobiography. He doesn't really want to believe too much in the significance of the manager (despite overwhelming survey evidence to the contrary, and although he might pay lip service to it because of corporate political correctness) because his own mythical life story tells him that he got to the top purely because of his own abilities, self-motivation and endeavour. Therefore, if people lower down the organization are not performing, it is not because of poor management, it is because those individuals are lazy or talentless. I did it, why can't they?

Another reason why those with real influence in large organizations are not sufficiently motivated to get management right is that they severely underestimate how bad management often is in practice. Firstly, this is because their personal experience of management is likely to have been more positive. Often a factor in their ascent to the top was the great luck that they had in having a good manager early on in their careers. This naturally colours their perception of general management standards.

Secondly, it is they themselves who will have selected the poor middle managers. If the managers they appointed are awful, what does that say about their own judgement? So they deny the truth to themselves and to others.

Lastly, many of them don't have the faintest clue what is happening in the lower reaches anyway and, one thing's for sure, nobody down there is going to make them any the wiser. The middle manager isn't going to put his hand up and say, 'hey, look at me, I'm really shit'; and none of his team are going to want to inflict on themselves the company equivalent of the Black Death, the label of 'troublemaker' (English translation: honest) rather than the much preferred 'team-player' (English translation: dishonest, jargon-spouting arse-licker). Bad news does not travel upwards in the corporate world.

A further cause of senior indifference to managerial standards is that promotion to middle management is currently a useful and convenient reward mechanism that can be used by those further up the ladder. Promotion to middle management is often the return for good performance in a functional role or for being the willing disciple of the Powerful Patron in the corporate political game. If you promote only potentially able managers, then how do you reward good functional performers and willing disciples?

Even if there is some intellectual appreciation among senior executives of the influence of middle managers on performance, and (here's the nub) how much do they as individuals honestly care about maximizing the potential of the company and the people within it? Many industries are dominated by an oligopoly, a small number of huge players who have carved up a large proportion of the potential client base between them. A few clients might move from one to another, but the reality is that many large companies, despite their desperate PR attempts to show that they operate in a highly innovative, cut-and-thrust, live-by-the-sword-die-by-the-sword environment, in fact occupy the business environment equivalent of a sleepy seaside town.

It is intense competition that stimulates the quest for efficiency, and maximizing the potential of all available human resources involves nothing less than excellent middle management. Without that intense competition, why should the Great Leaders care too much about the awful standard of their company's middle management and the resulting dissatisfaction down below? They will just continue to pick up their large bonus in the good years, their smaller bonus in the bad years, and all the while downstairs, they are playing poker on their computers and dreaming of 5.30 on Friday afternoon when they can go out and get pissed.

In the absence of too much external competition endangering their personal position, the principal anxiety of the Great Leaders will be internal threats. So even if they see the benefits of good management, why should they bother instituting a middle management constituency that is oriented towards the grass roots, and which therefore potentially will have the power created by popularity and influence? It's difficult enough now getting middle managers not to collude with the shop floor in ignoring grand strategies from on high. What would happen if they actually became popular? Outright rebellion could be on the cards.

Galvanizing the middle management task

If companies were really interested in excellence and therefore, good middle management, what would they do? First of all, they would radically redefine the role of the middle manager. The middle manager needs to be a talented people manager, not a downtrodden corporate functionary.

There are actually very few real managers currently in business. Mostly there are just 'managers' who set budgets, write the business plans that no one will read, sit around in the meaningless, jargon-filled meetings which are the pillar blocks of a corporate bureaucracy. The very term 'middle manager' has come to symbolize mediocrity, a pen-pusher who is going nowhere fast, who works long hours on mundane administrative tasks but is the most vulnerable at times of culling. But the middle manager, if the right people are selected for this role and they are employed correctly, is actually the most crucial figure in any company, for it is they who are (or should be) responsible for people management. For without the motivation, without the purpose, without the inspiration that can be instilled by their immediate supervisor, many will fall into, or actively seek out, the cracks that are the habitat/cemetery of the Living Dead.

The first major change required is that companies should seek to ensure, as far as is practically possible, that middle managers concentrate solely on people management, that they do nothing else whatsoever apart from this. People management is far too crucial a task not to demand full-time attention. In order to ensure that middle managers concentrate solely on organizing people, and on maximizing the potential contribution of those under their wing, they need to be remunerated purely on the strength of one indicator – the performance of their team set against previously defined targets. These targets will be more easily measurable in certain business environments than in others, but no team can prosper unless everyone in it clearly understands the precise goals it is striving for.

The main reason why so many middle managers do not currently pay sufficient attention to the people management for which they are nominally responsible is that it is seldom in their career interests to do so. Often, they will still be judged and remunerated, at least in part, for their performance in the functional role which they occupied previously, and despite promotion to management, continue to occupy. This naturally shifts the focus of the middle manager away from others and on to themselves. Moreover, this also provides a convenient pretext not to bother too much with the messy business of managing people. People are promoted to management almost always because they have performed well in their job. The reason they were good at their original job is probably that they enjoyed it and because of this, worked hard at it. When promoted, unless forced to abandon their previous role entirely, the inclination of most promoted managers will be to continue doing what they enjoy and ignore the difficult and awkward management bit.

The middle manager has also by now learned the rules of the corporate political game. There is more benefit in forming close relationships with those above, rather than with the impotent masses below. Further promotion up the corporate ladder depends now on gambling on which Powerful Patron is most likely to rise further up the ranks of the Great Leaders, and then cosying up beside them. But clearly, the more time the middle manager spends looking up, the less time is spent looking down. Making pay completely dependent on team results would transfer a great deal of the manager's attention to those who need it.

Identifying middle management potential

Making managerial pay dependent on team performance would also provide the added bonus of assisting in changing the methods used in pinpointing those with management potential. Currently any ambitious individual who wants to ascend the corporate heights needs to become a middle manager of some sort. If that individual is asked in an internal interview whether they want to manage others, their rational, but usually utterly dishonest answer is, 'oh yes, I see that as a great challenge, but one that I would relish and which I am confident I would be good at'. And then they get promoted, become an awful, or just absent, manager (not that anyone above them cares particularly) and then seek to work their way further up the system.

If managers were really judged purely by their managerial performance, you would eliminate that dishonesty overnight. And it *is* dishonesty. How many of us really do want to manage other people? How many of us want to deal every day, as every manager has to, with the ultra-ambitious, the lazy, the backstabbers, the liars, the snide, the arrogant. It is a rare breed of person who actually is prepared to endure all of this, just for the potential thrill of extracting the best out of others. It is no wonder that so many promoted managers avoid managing at all possible costs. Don't blame them, blame the system that incentivizes them to assume managerial responsibility when they don't honestly want it, and couldn't manage others anyway even if their lives depended on it.

Rather than the predictable question and answer we currently get in interviews for first-time management positions, we should get the following: 'OK Jim/Helen, you are good at your job, you are ambitious, you want to get on. All good stuff. You say you want to manage. But do you really want to give up absolutely everything you have done before in your job and take up a position that involves dealing with people all day, and where the pay will depend completely on the performance of others?' I am confident that at least 95% of people would run out of the room screaming at this point. As being very good at anything in life requires at the very least the strong urge to do it, the remaining 5% might just have a chance of being a good manager. Just by changing the way managers are judged and remunerated, you will have made the management selection process far easier and also far more effective. Before you enter the complex phase of assessing potential ability to manage, you will have eliminated the mass of managerial no-hopers.

How do we select the best potential managers from the remaining 5%? There are several innate characteristics of the able people manager. The most important is the extremely rare trait of a developed perceptiveness about other people. This characteristic enables the manager to identify quickly the strengths and weaknesses of others and how best to motivate different types of individual. It is quite possible to have this perceptiveness without the passion to manage (there are plenty of writers, artists and analysts who have an acute understanding of people, but perhaps sometimes because of this, have no desire to spend much time with them), in which case the ability to manage well will still be beyond reach.

The extreme rarity of managerial perceptiveness consigns many with ability to a career of perpetual underperformance and possible Living Death. In their book *The Set-Up-to-Fail Syndrome: How Good Managers Cause Great People to Fail*, INSEAD academics Jean-Francois Manzoni and Jean-Louis Barsoux detail the destructive impact of the moment when a manager arrives at the quick, and often unjustified, conclusion that a particular employee lacks 'the right stuff'. This then sets off a vicious spiral.

After research that covers interviews and surveys among 3,000 employees and executives in a broad range of companies, they concluded that 'once people are miscast as weaker performers, they tend to live down to that image, regardless of their capabilities'. Studies in numerous settings indicate that the performance of individuals fluctuates according to the expectations of powerful others, such as teachers and bosses. Whatever their true potential, people's resistance to low expectations is short-lived. Now with diminished self-belief, the employee lacks the opportunity to change the boss's mindset because the latter will not trust them with challenging work. Thus a classic Catch-22 situation develops, leading to a self-reinforcing cycle of bitterness and blame.

Manzoni and Barsoux were doubtless anxious not to offend their potential readership, as they included the phrase 'good managers' in their sub-title. Managers are not 'good' if they routinely let able people rot. They are awful managers who should be removed from their job immediately before they wreak more damage on their business and on people's lives. Managers must be directly accountable for the underperformance of any of their team. They must look in the mirror before anything else. As Peter Drucker, the management author, once said: 'The productivity of work is not the responsibility of the worker but of the manager.'

The passion to manage and perceptiveness can no more be learned or taught than can a love of cricket or artistic talent. Management training has been created not as a means to improve management but because certain constituencies, and certainly not the managed, benefit from it. Clearly the most vocal proponent of management training is the seller. A whole industry of management training, sparked and perpetuated by the management books of the Esteemed Gurus (themselves the greatest beneficiaries of the training industry), has grown out of the pretence that innate characteristics, or deeply held personal inclinations and passions, can be instilled through sitting in a room for two days listening to hackneyed jargon.

There would be no industry, though, without willing buyers. Many of the senior executives who decide on training investments don't honestly believe in the merit of management training. If they did, it wouldn't be the first thing to be cut when the business climate starts getting tough. Many, because of personal prejudice, their vested interest in the status quo or their detachment from reality, don't really see the pressing need to improve management standards anyway. If they were genuinely interested in management excellence, any training purchased would not merely focus on attempting to squeeze the square peg of an uninspiring, unpopular and uninterested manager into a round hole. Rather it would concentrate on teaching senior executives how to revolutionize the role of the middle manager, how to avoid continuing to participate in hugely destructive middle management selection, and how to go about the onerous and crucial task of choosing the best potential managers in their organization in the first place.

Too much management training presently attempts, pointlessly, to shut the stable door after the horse has bolted. It too often presents a convenient method of making companies appear to their staff, and to external observers and watchdogs, that they care about management standards, without offering the radical rethink that so many companies need, but which is deeply threatening to those who benefit from the current system. In other words, it is largely a sop. It ticks the necessary boxes but usually serves little purpose.

 confused

What about the career background of first-time middle managers? As they should immediately abandon the functional role previously occupied upon promotion to middle management, their past performance in that role is in fact wholly irrelevant when it comes to considering them for a management position. The management skill is far more rare than functional expertise, and requires entirely different qualities.

Businesses have not cottoned on to this. A survey by the human resources consultancy DDI from 2005 showed that present-day captains of industry were often star pupils at school. Of the 105 business leaders interviewed, 70% were prefects, 50% had captained a sports team and 30% were a head or deputy head of a school. In the wake of the report, Lucy McGee, a director of DDI, explained the rationale for the survey: 'We wanted to find out who the really good leaders were and what characteristics they shared. There is a huge leadership shortage in business, and this could help companies know where to look.' This is all self-contradictory. The general standard of management is awful, as McGee herself suggests, and therefore business must be getting it wrong by promoting these high achievers without sufficient thought. Just because someone is fiercely ambitious and very able at school and in their early careers, it does not follow that they will make good managers. Indeed, it could mean that they are so concerned with their own achievements that they will not be interested in anyone else's.

Functional expertise requires an aptitude for the role, and a willingness to work hard at it. Managerial excellence necessitates a hunger to manage and perceptiveness about people, among other attributes. Being good at either the functional role or managing doesn't preclude being good at the other, but nor is there any intrinsic relationship between the two, as the history of sport clearly demonstrates. Being a great basketball player won't make you a great basketball coach, the fact that you are a great football manager doesn't mean you were a great football player, being a great cook doesn't mean you play the violin well. It is a self-evident truth that people are good at different things, that they work harder at different things, but because it suits companies to reward able performers with promotion to management, this elementary logic is seldom followed in the corporate world.

Management tomorrow

Once a successful middle manager is found, what then do we do with them? If good managers are both crucially important for companies and also extremely scarce, how do we keep them managing? Ambitious individuals who perform well in their jobs naturally want more money and status. They want to move into the ranks of the Great Leaders. That's where the money is, the status, the power.

Currently, many of those who enter the top positions are not the best able to perform in them. Even when competition forces meritocracy to take a firmer grip, there will be many more people who have the strategic mind and the imagination necessary to be a truly effective senior executive than there will be those who have the people skills necessary to be an excellent middle manager. (You could of course say that senior executives have people management responsibilities too. But when you get to a certain level, the people in your team will usually be safe company men who are lodged so far up your backside that management becomes something of a walk in the park, albeit because of this, a slightly uncomfortable one.)

This is really a fundamental paradox at the heart of large corporates: essential and rare managerial talent is rewarded with much less pay and status than easily replaceable leaders whose direct influence is highly over-rated anyway. In time the effects of competition will inevitably address this irrational imbalance. (All this is not to say that senior executives will not have a vital role in the competitive world of the future, but just that they will never be as important as middle managers. Indeed, as we shall see later, one of the main tasks for those senior executives who are genuinely interested in addressing the plague of sluggishness in their organization will be to look to reduce their own power and to transfer more control to the company's constituent units.)

As business is exposed to the effects of globalization and therefore, increased competition, it will be gradually forced to improve performance. This slowly accelerating drive for improved efficiency will create the need for more internal transparency, to measure exactly who is contributing what within the organization. This transparency will in turn serve to dem-onstrate ever more clearly the considerable benefits of the able manager. More and more surveys that establish the strong link between individual performance and the influence of the immediate supervisor will also be published. As competition heats up, companies will be forced, against their will, to act on all this evidence, and the status and pay of the able middle manager will rise accordingly.

The lessons of sport are especially instructive as we look to the future of business management. As sport has over the years become increas-ingly competitive, and the need to succeed more intense, the significance attached to the manager has grown, just as it inevitably will grow in business as it itself becomes more and more competitive, transparent and professional. In this way, sport does not only provide lessons for manage-ment because of its openness and the simple measurability of performance, it is also a precursor and predictor of future organizational priorities in business. Professional sport is always the pinnacle of competition. That really is its essential appeal, the reason why so many people love watching it. Competition always stimulates the quest for efficiency, and sport has discovered that efficiency necessitates the right managers to be painstakingly sought out.

It is no coincidence that the profile of Rugby Union team managers has dramatically increased since it turned professional in the 1990s. Rugby Union previously had the image of a game that was there simply to be enjoyed by its participants, and if you won the game, it was a bonus. Not so now, hence the need for a talented manager. A similar process has occurred within cricket. Until recently, the England national team would have a chairman of selectors and a playing captain. The need to maximize individual and team performance in a harder, more aggressive playing environment has resulted in the appointment of a full-time manager with a proven track record of success.

Perhaps the clearest example of this trend towards the recognition of the power of the manager has occurred within football. Before the 1920s, teams didn't have managers. The chairman and board of directors would decide the make-up of the team. The potential positive effect of having a single individual at the helm with real managerial talent only became apparent with the arrival on the scene of Herbert Chapman, the first great modern manager.

Now, ambitious football clubs know that they cannot hope to get the best from their playing staff unless they get the right manager. The top managers are highly paid and much coveted by competing clubs, the more so because football has also learned another lesson which business hasn't – good management is extremely rare. This realization within football has taken root to such an extent that managerial selections which would have been unthinkable even a generation ago, even a decade ago, are now becoming commonplace in British football. Firstly, foreign managers arrived. And now, increasingly, foreign managers who can barely speak a word of English. What football is effectively admitting with these appointments is that the skill of management is so rare, innate and unlearnable that it is far easier to learn a foreign language from scratch than to become a good manager. It is surely only a matter of time, as the pressures to succeed become more intense and the appreciation of the scarcity of management talent untainted by failure grows still further, that the trend moves one step further and successful managers from other sports are given the opportunity to try their luck in football.

Even if it doesn't want to, the corporate world will inevitably follow the same path as the more advanced world of sport. At dinner parties in the future, when asked what they do for a living, there will be those who respond that they are a 'manager' or whatever the buzzword is for a manager at that time. The industry they work in will be irrelevant, because the talented manager will be able to sell his services across the full spectrum of industries. Learning the fundamentals of a new business isn't difficult, but you can't learn to be a good manager. The days of the morale-sapping managerial incompetent will soon be numbered. The future is extremely bright for those in business whose sole ability and ambition is to manage other people, irrespective of how bad they are at doing their job, or how little they suck up to their superiors.

જી

CHAPTER 7

AUTOPSY AND RESURRECTION

'80% of success is showing up.'

Woody Allen

A pologists for absenteeism argue that it is often caused by stress as a result of overwork, and anyway the far bigger problem is the health risk of people bowing down to the pervasive culture of 'presenteeism', by turning up for work when they are sick just because they fear the repercussions if they don't. That is, their employers run such conscienceless sweatshops that people's chances of getting through the week without getting sacked can be severely endangered by acting like a Southern party-frock and staying in bed for an extra couple of hours with a spot of terminal cancer. So they just keep taking the diamorphine and struggle in to participate in the chaotically hectic rat race until they finally keel over and die, becoming just another notch on the bed post of evil, insatiable capitalism.

And it won't be long before they do die, according to research by University College London. A team investigated the fitness and attendance records of 10,000 Whitehall staff over ten years, and concluded that between 30 and 40% of those who continued to work when ill, even when afflicted by a minor complaint such as the common cold, later suffered twice the rate of heart disease. The head of the survey, Professor Sir Michael Marmot, stressed the dangers exposed by the findings: 'So many people force themselves into work when they are not well and have little knowledge of the consequences. Far from contributing to their companies or spreading a few germs around the office, they could be hastening their own death.' Words which were music to the ears of a spokesman for The Public and Commercial Sector Union who called for a more 'inventive' way to deal with absenteeism: 'The big stick approach seems to be in vogue at the moment but this survey shows it is not beneficial for anyone.'

So which should concern us more, absenteeism or presenteeism? The answer is that the very fact that we are discussing either should concern anyone interested in the level of productivity in our offices. The debate about both subjects reveals our excessive interest in an individual's physical whereabouts. Absent from what? Present at what? At a place of work? So what if people are present at work? When did you last meet a company shareholder who cared how many hours employees spend in the office?

The office roll-call

We need to look beyond the statistics on absenteeism and presenteeism and think more carefully about what they signify. Dishonest absenteeism in itself may cost billions, but its significance is far broader and more serious. If considerable numbers of office workers think nothing of phoning in sick when they are perfectly healthy, what does that mean they are doing when they are actually at work? They don't suddenly transform themselves from malingerers to productive workers just because their physical being happens to be located in the office. This is convincingly borne out by statistics detailed in this book.

Certain companies have adopted measures to thwart absenteeism. Tesco and the removal company Pickfords do not pay workers for the first three days off sick, in an attempt to combat absenteeism through faked illness. Pickfords have also introduced a system whereby a worker who wants to take the day off sick now has to call a trained nurse at a specialist healthcare company. Pickfords' human resources manager, Stephen Fellows, explained the logic behind the move: 'An individual who is not actually sick but is claiming to be sick might well be deterred by having to speak to somebody who is medically trained.' The company claims to have cut absenteeism by 30% through this strategy.

And this success will be a real boon for Pickfords. When a worker turns up, he will be employed in a team of removal men doing physical work, the measurement of which will be simple – how many removals they performed, how big are the houses in question, or whatever. So if a worker turns up, he will be working, and if he isn't working, his colleagues and his employer will soon have something to say about it.

But most office jobs in the service sector are far more amorphous and less measurable. The use of trained nurses might also be a clever method of curbing dishonest absenteeism in offices, but the overall effect is unlikely to be an increase in productivity. It's too easy to hide in the office itself. You can do a good job of coercing physical presence in an office, but why bother if the same demotivated people who were faking illness just fake work instead? And that's if they have to fake it. There are plenty who don't work, and don't really feel the need to make any effort to hide the fact.

Many people, mostly men, wear the macho badge of pride about always making it into work: 'Thirty-seven years and I haven't missed a day's work, even the day after I had both my legs sawn off by a vicious psychopath.' Yes, great, well done. But what did you actually do in those thirty-seven years? Despite my six months' productive work in six years, I myself never once took a day off dishonestly. But, as my story earlier in the book recounts, my presence in the office was usually so pointless that my employer even forgot I existed for the best part of a year.

Presenteeism reveals the average worker's ridiculous but often all too accurate understanding of the psychological contract with his employer. It is the turning up that is the priority, not the productivity. You can often get away with doing next to nothing in the office for years, but a week off work without a sufficiently convincing excuse and you could be on the midnight train to Dolesville. That is not to say that the latter is acceptable. Of course it isn't. But the contrast in the reaction of the employer reveals so much about what is fundamentally wrong with our whole mindset with respect to 'work'.

This psychological contract does not come from nowhere. It emanates from the physical, legal contract that stipulates an employee's place of 'work' and hours of 'work' but frequently elucidates little about the work that needs to be performed, apart from an often meaningless job title. It represents a legacy from earlier days in the industrial era when presence and productivity were synonymous. If a worker was located by his machine in the factory, productivity would be the inevitable result.

Indeed, the word 'work' is interesting in itself. It is too rarely used for its principal meaning – 'to exert oneself physically or mentally in order to do, make, or accomplish something'. More frequently, it is used as a concrete noun signifying a visible object, the place of work, as in 'today I'm going to work, where I'm going to do f**k all as usual.' Or, alternatively, as an abstract noun: 'How was work this week?' people routinely ask. What do they mean when they ask this? In this sense, 'work' incorporates so many different facets – the relationship with your work colleagues, with your boss, your journey to and from your place of work, any progress in your standing in the office hierarchy, any social activities with colleagues, and so on. In short, 'work' encompasses the entire experience of the rituals of office life, of which the level of productive output is but one, often insignificant, detail. ('It must take great self-discipline to sit down and make yourself work every day', office workers say to me when I tell them that I have been writing a book. This comment, the most common reaction when I tell people what I am doing, is particularly revealing. Aren't they supposed to be working as well?)

It is not productivity that seems to be important to the employer, and the employee intuitively understands this. Appearing to work is more important than working, presence of body more important than presence of mind. Sick people do not go in to offices, as the unions and left-wing commentators would have us believe, because they are pushed to the limit by an uncaring employer and have mountains of work to get through. They go in because they do not want to be seen to be physically absent. People might argue that they would feel guilty if they didn't go in, and this therefore indicates their conscientiousness. But it doesn't. It merely emphasizes the farcical importance attached to physical presence. Would they feel the same guilt if they turned up and did nothing?

Going into the office when sick is one manifestation of presenteeism. The other is the 'long hours' office culture of certain service industries. Again, productivity takes a back seat to physical presence. 'I'm an early bird, always in the office before 7a.m.' is another pointless phrase, saying much more about the speaker's desire to appear industrious than about productivity. The tendency of the ambitious in the corporate world to work long hours is rooted in the psychological (and indeed the legal) contract between employee and employer.

Because 'work' is defined as hours spent in an office, we have gone along unthinkingly with the superficially logical but utterly misleading view that long hours must mean performing work above and beyond the call of duty. 'We don't have a nine to five culture around here' is often the proud boast of interviewer to interviewee, or of the experienced hand to the novice on his first day in the office. This comment is supposed to tease or frighten the youngster, indicating an intimidating culture of hard work (and principally of course, implying that the bosses themselves, including the speaker, are not afraid of getting their hands dirty). But as always in the world of the office, you need to look beyond the words to extract the real meaning.

For a lawyer or other professionals who charge out services by the hour, the long hours they put in will have a direct impact on their company's profitability. But in the majority of office jobs where output is difficult to measure, where the job description is nebulous and the management does not take a detailed interest in employee output, long hours are in the main an overt political statement, another demonstration of the conformity necessary to attain individual success in the corporate world, rather than evidence of hard work. And when a critical mass of people participate in this sham, it gradually becomes unacceptable for others to abstain, thus creating a self-perpetuating and comical company or industry culture where thousands of people spend long hours every day not working at 'work'.

Statistics on long hours are repeatedly used to demonstrate overwork and stress. But overwork is not the same as long hours. Indeed, a culture of long hours can frequently indicate a low level of performance measurability, which will inevitably result overall in underwork, rather than overwork. There would be no point working long hours if it were immediately apparent that little work is being performed. And if a working culture is sufficiently opaque that working late in the evening for no demonstrable purpose benefits one's career, then it will also be opaque enough for the same person to do nothing in the morning and afternoon, provided he looked busy. Lack of transparency creates the conditions for image to triumph over performance.

If there is stress involved in long hours, it is not the stress directly caused by working long hours. As the surveys detailed earlier in the book conclude, workplace stress is principally the result of the office politics that spawns the long hours culture in the first place. Long hours and stress are not father and son. Indeed, long hours, stress and workplace inactivity are all siblings – the offspring of the office politics caused by a lack of transparency in the system, the fact that nobody really has a clue what anyone else is up to.

Home advantage

One way to combat this lack of transparency is, paradoxically, to remove the office employee from view altogether, by ensuring that they work from home on a regular basis.

Opponents of home working within the corporate world might argue that it is more difficult to manage home workers and to monitor their performance. But the opposite is true. Dishonesty may hold sway in the office. But as soon as an employee works from home, his contribution, or lack of it, will not be camouflaged by the meretricious practices of the office, the staying late for no purpose, the jacket over the chair, being seen talking to the right people, contributing to pointless meetings with impressive-sounding but empty words. You've been at home for a few days – tell me exactly what you've done and what it contributes to the business.

Home working shifts the emphasis from presence to work. It forces everyone concerned to refocus their attention on why people are employed to do jobs in the first place. 'I work hard. I get up at 5.30 a.m. and commute for two hours each way to get into work', says the office employee, thinking that getting up early and travelling for hours is evidence of their commitment and toil. It isn't, it just shows how far they have to travel to be present in the office. Take that commute away, and the same employee has to confront the stark truth that it is consistent hard work that is proof of conscientiousness, not uncomfortable and time-consuming journeys to a place of work.

There are genuine drawbacks to home working, the principal one being that if a worker is not in the office it becomes more difficult for them to build up the positive relationship with a manager, which is so conducive to motivation and productivity. For that reason, full-time home working for the office employee might not be the simple panacea for low levels of productivity. But very regular home working should not just be a perk for relatively senior staff. (According to the UK Labour Force Survey of 2002, there are twice as many tele-working managers as administrative staff, a statistic that clearly reveals the widespread corporate fear that the average worker cannot be properly controlled at home.) It should be introduced at all levels as a positive strategy to boost performance, by reminding everyone that wearing a suit while sitting in an office after a long commute does not constitute work.

Home working presents a threat to the Professional Operator by confiscating the tools of office posturing, which he needs to be able to prosper. Indeed, the reason why home working has not exploded in the way predicted in many quarters after the sudden proliferation of electronic communication is not just because of employer reservations. Many workers will fear the nakedness of home working and what it might reveal about their usefulness. For those without that particular insecurity, freedom from the office means working hard to complete a series of tasks, followed by time spent with family and friends, or pursuing personal interests, or serving the community in other ways, rather than by time-filling meetings surrounded by people who by a quirk of fate happen to be employed by the same company, and then an hour and a half spent sitting on the 6.12 from Paddington.

More home working would be of particular benefit to women. Firstly, because it affords them the flexibility which many of them want or need in order to combine work with domestic responsibilities (see the next chapter). And secondly, because it removes the roots of male corporate success and female corporate failure. There is no clubby chumminess in home working, there are no backslapping and beers after work, there are no discussions about Saturday's controversial refereeing decision, or about the 20-foot putt which won the company golf day. Home working centres on demonstrable work, and all the peripheral and time-wasting office activities that men use to climb the ladder become irrelevant.

Business development consultancy

In her tongue-in-cheek advice to people who want to do nothing at work, Corinne Maier suggests seeking 'positions in which your progress is impossible to determine: a highly specialized technical post nobody else understands, or an area so vast, such as "integration of anti-discriminatory strategies", that success cannot be determined'.

The only people who do any work in large companies, Maier claims, are 'either at the operational end of the company – the mail room, the sales people – or on short-term contracts who are paid according to the number of set tasks they achieve. This little army of workers is supporting a whole superstructure of people with long titles and not much to do'. 'I mean', she goes on, 'what exactly is a compliance manager? A quality control manager? A corporate social responsibility officer? What do they produce that's tangible, and who's holding them to account?'

Much has been written in the right-wing press about obscure and unaccountable jobs in the public sector. Writing in the *Daily Mail* in September 2002, Edward Heathcoat Amory railed against the abundance of vague-sounding jobs financed by the tax payer: 'The Society section of the *Guardian* is not advertising for nurses and the like. Instead, pages are packed with expensive ads for consultation officers, social workers, outreach workers, ethnic minority project leaders, travel plan co-ordinators, strategy managers, health and fitness officers ... the list goes on and on.' These jobs contribute nothing, says Heathcoat Amory: 'Too many of these roles are essentially parasitic, feeding off the real economy and involving form-filling, memo-writing and back-covering. They are magnets for those seeking the cushy billet, perfect for individuals adept at filling out forms, firing off memos and covering their backs.'

The *Daily Mail* might want to believe that the dynamic, ruthlessly efficient and ultra-competitive private sector is paying hand over fist for the soft public-sector underbelly, incorporating all those lovely state-sponsored jobs for the boys. And in the case of the many hard-pressed independent traders and small businesses, struggling to maintain profit margins to keep afloat, the newspaper is right. But as Maier stresses, and anyone who has opened their eyes when working for their own large company will know, the private sector is also packed full of jobs which contribute little of substance, and which thereby divert funds away from where they should be, in the hands of company shareholders or invested in growing the company and creating useful jobs, which themselves in turn lead to sustained growth and profitability.

Unless in a job that they feel genuinely passionate about, anyone employed in a role in which performance is either not easily measurable, or alternatively not frequently assessed in detail, will simply do the rational thing. They will use the little intellect necessary to ensure that they give the impression that they are contributing, while performing the least amount of genuine work possible. And this *is* rational behaviour, just as rational as the small businessman working all hours to make ends meet, or an entrepreneur racking his brains to dream up an idea that will sell.

Employees in large offices who are not clearly accountable understand instinctively that they are paid to occupy a position, not to perform demonstrable and useful work. Those who attain higher pay realize that they do so because they occupy a more senior position or because they happen to occupy a position in an industry with more profits sloshing around, not necessarily because they produce more indispensable work. Workers might not be able to articulate this idea, and may not even want to admit this personally degrading reality to themselves, but they know it deep down. Human beings are remarkably alert to what they need to do to put food on the table. People always adapt to the market, and the market currently pays millions of people to be at their desk from nine to five (or nine to nine), whether they produce anything of economic value or not.

಄

Non-jobs happen for a variety of reasons. Firstly, insufficient thought might have gone into considering what the job entails and whether it really is necessary before someone is recruited. The role will be created on the impetuous and unchecked whim of an individual invested with the authority to recruit. If it is not a front-line sales role, the job description drawn up is likely to be woolly and inscrutable, with goals and targets imprecise and immeasurable. If you remain unconvinced that such positions are in abundance in the private sector, go to the Appointments section of the broadsheet press.

This hiring will take place when the business cycle is favourable, for there will be long periods in more inauspicious times in the life of the corporate, or in the wake of a merger or acquisition, when there is a freeze or a severe cutback on recruitment. This period will generally also involve people being made redundant from their jobs. But don't assume that the most ineffectual roles will be eradicated in these culls. It is likely that the same lack of thought will go into selecting which jobs should go as that which went into the original recruitment. The inability to measure contribution will result in the exit of those who failed to foster the most advantageous political alliances, or those who are just plain unlucky. If the decree is that 10% should go, that 10% will comprise a broad spectrum of the able and the mediocre, the useful and the presently useless.

Non-jobs comprise the superfluous as well as the plain pointless. In boom times, a recruiter might double the size of a team of individuals who are all performing the same role, in order to meet the growing customer demand. When market conditions subside, the team is overmanned. A smaller, nimbler and better-organized company might react appropriately to changing circumstance. In the fog of the large corporate, where nobody really knows what anyone else does, excessive staffing levels may well persist throughout the downturn in the business cycle. A team of ten continues to do the job that a team of three could now do. The unwieldiness of the organization, and its resulting low level of responsiveness, prevent the remaining seven from being temporarily repositioned more profitably or removed from the wage bill entirely.

Recruitment might also be used as a political tool. Recent academic research in the United States lends weight to the argument that undertaking company acquisitions might appeal to senior executives because the empires they build increase their personal standing and prestige in the business community. Similarly, those further down the ladder might be inclined to augment the number of their subordinates because a bigger team makes them seem more influential and powerful internally within the company, not because increased staffing is necessary to perform the relevant work.

Politics also results in the retention of the unproductive but well connected. As advantageous relationships might take years to generate, and will more often than not involve those in a position to reciprocate political favours, this constituency will consist pretty much entirely of the senior and hence relatively well paid, thus costing the company dear.

Right person, wrong job

As surveys detailed previously in the book indicate, there are large numbers of people who are plain dissatisfied and disillusioned with their work. It is simply impossible for someone who is intrinsically bored by their job to devote themselves to it, day in, day out, year in, year out. A few weeks maybe, even a few months for the more stoical among us, but much more is surely beyond all of us. So, in time, even if they spend long hours at their desk to keep up appearances, the bored will increasingly seek ways to avoid work, a goal that is entirely possible in a large office environment. In the absence of a management tier dedicated to people, identifying the demotivated and perhaps rekindling their enthusiasm in a role more suited to their abilities and preferences, they are simply left to drift, contributing nothing but their infectious cynicism.

Recent Gallup research, examining interviews with more than 1.4 million employees in many countries, confirms the inverse relationship between length of service and employee engagement. People might start off their new jobs with a feeling of optimism, but slowly but surely reality returns to remind them why they left their last job in the first place. While the percentage of engaged workers in the first year of service nears 40%, that percentage decreases to an average of little more than 20% for the period between three and ten years of service. 'For most employees', Gallup report, 'the first year on the job is their best. It's downhill from there for the worker and for the company as well, because disengaged employees are a drag on profit and sales and overall satisfaction among customers.'

The researchers admit to being surprised by the results: 'We expected to see an increasing sense of belonging over time. New hires, we figured, would be tentative, unsure of what to expect from their jobs, their managers and their co-workers. But as time passed, we assumed that uncertainty would diminish and companies would see engagement ratings rise as managers helped new workers identify their talents, learn skills and move into roles that drew upon their particular strengths. But that's not what happens.' So much for the idea that longevity indicates commitment and loyalty. More often, it merely signals an acceptance of boredom, a long-term trade-off of position occupation for financial security, or indicates an energy-sapping despondency that has prevented the employee from seeking to escape his rut by finding other, more enjoyable, ways to make a living.

Mistakes are inevitably made after the superficial and frequently deceptive interview process. People are always going to be hired for the wrong jobs (a survey published on hrlook.com in early 2005 reported that 75% of employers are not confident that they will choose the right applicant when they're hiring). Plenty of very capable people, for example, are frequently appointed to roles in business production or sales when they simply don't possess the proactive bent required to build a portfolio of clients from scratch, or to creative positions requiring the type of imagination they just don't have.

What is unforgivable is that those mistakes are not rectified, and that the stagnant, unreactive environment of the large office allows those same people to saunter unnoticed into the world of the Living Dead. And if there is a proven direct relationship between longevity and loss of engagement, UK government statistics do not offer succour. Despite the popularly held notion that we have already entered an unprecedented period of carefree job-hopping and employee versatility, a larger percentage of the employed had been in their jobs for more than ten years in 2000 (31%), than had been in 1986 (29%) (Office for National Statistics).

Even if an individual's strengths and interests do match the position, all but those with the most limited horizons and the least imagination are going to become a little jaded after doing the same job for a number of years. In this way, the passage of time all but guarantees that a good fit between individual and job eventually ceases to be so productive. If that individual is influential enough to engineer his own internal transfer at the time when the boredom sets in, all well and good. But for most others, despite the standard corporate boast of an open and flexible working culture where individual opportunities simply need to be seen and grasped, any request to change roles will generally be viewed as the actions of an awkward troublemaker. 'Who is this guy, forcing me to waste my time paying attention to mere underlings? Does he seriously want me to remove my head from my own boss's backside and actually do some managing? He should be grasping his own opportunities anyway. That's the way we do things here.' Many of the most energetic and ambitious will seek to escape their career cul-de-sac by attempting to reinvigorate their career, temporarily at least, in a different environment.

According to a poll by TalentMax, the talent management specialists, 86% of financial services organizations admitted that reluctance or inability to address career planning with employees leads to the loss of good people. Much more regular switching of roles would undoubtedly act as a counter to boredom and drift. But very powerful mechanisms work against this more effective deployment of human resources. First, the gross indifference of abysmal managers who are not paid to manage anyway. Second, the huge barriers to entry that exist to protect those currently reaping the benefits of position occupation in a particular industry or role. Anyone who has tried changing career direction will have had their enthusiasm dampened by reading all those job advertisements demanding several years' experience in a similar role as a prerequisite. Every industry, it seems, prefers the tired, ossifying contribution of those imbued with deep-set prejudice to the enthusiasm engendered by novelty and to freshness of perspective.

It is not difficult to learn the necessary fundamentals of all but the most technical of industries and roles. Still, the myth persists that industry insiders possess mountains of esoteric knowledge that would take years for the average Joe to grasp. The myth is reinforced by the intimidating jargon that every industry constructs in order to frighten off pesky outsiders who might have their eyes set on derailing their gravy train. 'You never stop learning in this industry.' Bollocks, unless of course you have particularly severe learning difficulties. 'I've got twenty years' experience in this game.' Six months learning, and nineteen years and six months scratching my arse.

The Channel 4 programme *Faking It*, where a contestant is given four weeks to learn a skill well enough to fool a panel of 'expert' judges, must make thoroughly depressing viewing for those whose self-esteem derives solely from having mastered the expertise featured. Week after week, contestants manage to dupe the judges that they are an experienced TV director or chef, or whatever. If the producers of the programme were to devote a series to various white-collar office industries, a losing contestant would become an even rarer event. But in the real world, the benefits of job switching for individual workers and for our economy are passed over, losing out to the instincts of insecurity and self-preservation of insiders seeking to cling on to their meal ticket.

Millions could escape their prison cell of tedium and torpor by means of a new style of job market which offers them the opportunity to add variety to their working lives. But first we have to recognize the truth and maybe, in doing so, accept a blow to the personal pride emanating from career success. Most jobs are easy.

Size does matter

There will always be considerable levels of inactivity in a large company, no matter what the industry. The principal reason for this is that there is simply a greater proportion of people in large companies who have no interest in their work.

Gallup conducted a survey measuring engagement levels at both small and large companies. Their conclusion was that employees become less engaged as a company's workforce grows. Engagement, the feeling of being fully involved with one's job, was highest (33% of employees) at companies with fewer than 50 workers. Furthermore, at companies with 1000 to 5000 employees, 19% feel 'actively disengaged', or fundamentally disconnected from their work, versus 12% at companies with fewer than 50 workers.

Gallup researchers attribute the higher engagement of small company employees to their greater sense of 'local control', 'the feeling of connection to, and accountability for, company output'. In larger companies, 'hierarchy and bureaucracy can make employees feel their contributions don't matter'.

The effects of this disconnection will also be more pronounced in a larger company. Whereas demotivated employees in a smaller company might be forced to knuckle down because people will notice if they don't, their counterparts in a larger company will find it far easier to avoid doing the work that they so despise, and which deprives them of any sense of meaning and achievement. So the greater level of disengagement in larger companies produces a disproportionately negative outcome, as the inactive can get away with it for years. (This is not to mention of course the large band of do-nothing, but probably quite engaged, Professional Operators, to whom a large company is as water to a duck).

The same Gallup survey also stresses that employees of larger companies actually intend to stay there longer, despite the lower levels of engagement, thereby further compounding the effects of this disengagement. 61% of those who work for companies with less than 50 employees plan to be with their company one year from now, compared with 64% of those in companies with more than 1000 employees. It's boring, and it gets more boring each year, but I don't really have to do anything, the benefits are good, and I'm going to have to put my kids through university soon, so let's not look a gift horse in the mouth, shall we?

To address the malaise in larger companies, Gallup suggests learning from small company practices: 'To replicate the local control of small companies, managers at large companies should bear in mind that some work units within an organization can be engaged at the small-company level.' Wherever possible, in other words, break large companies and large departments down into small teams made up of individuals with a loyalty to each other, a commitment to the agreed and clear goals of that particular team which they are incentivized, without ambiguity, to achieve and with one manager dedicated to extracting the best out of the collective whole and its constituent individuals. The most apparently boring tasks can suddenly become engaging, once the individual acquires a genuine personal interest in the standard of their work, either by working for themselves or for a team to which they are committed. Forget loyalty and commitment to the wider company. In an organization of a certain size, it simply won't and can't exist; not at the grass roots anyway.

As always with teams, the selection of the manager is crucial (see previous chapter), as Gallup acknowledges: 'In work units of fewer than 10 people ... engagement will soar or plummet depending on the manager. That's because in small groups, each member keenly feels a good manager's ability to communicate and motivate – and a bad manager's incompetence. So if you expect your teams to be top-performing, make sure your managers are up to the challenge.'

The only way large companies can cure the plague of the Living Death is by religiously chopping and dividing until the company comprises hundreds, if not thousands, of self-contained units, each run by talented managers who want to do nothing but manage, and whose remuneration depends purely on verifiable managerial success. This will not solve the problem entirely, as there are many lost in the woodwork of the large company who work in a vague but isolated role, which would not fit easily into the framework of a team. These positions really need to be constantly assessed, and discontinued whenever their value to the business becomes difficult to ascertain and quantify. Moreover, there will be many in the higher reaches who would undoubtedly use their wiles and influence to ensure that their lack of contribution is not permanently exposed by being placed in the illuminating environment of a small team, where every action is open to scrutiny from the manager and colleagues. But a move towards many more small self-contained teams would go a long way towards combating large company sluggishness and inertia.

The problem is that this path will also lead to a loss of central control. How can you offer local control to hundreds of units, as Gallup suggests, when there is one overall corporate strategy that needs to be followed? Surely one of the features of local control must be the drawing up of goals and methods of operating which all the members of that small team buy into and agree to aspire towards. But no senior management team that intends to run a company of 50,000 people from the centre can cope with small groups of ten people each going off in their separate chosen directions. The answer surely lies in first dividing the larger company into several separate company units, each with its own very distinct strategy and totally independent control, and only then breaking down the respective units into the small teams. The presence of these teams will be more compatible with a much smaller company unit, just because fifty self-contained teams are more manageable than five thousand.

Increasing motivation levels in large companies thus involves decentralization of power. A monolithic corporate structure might offer the mirage of control (and also the often overestimated possibilities of cross-selling of company products), but you cannot control the minds of the bored thousands who turn up just to get their pay cheque and who then direct their energies and talents towards doing nothing. The day of their Second Coming, and the leap in productivity which will accompany it, will only be made possible by replicating the dynamic and transparent environment of a small company, and then installing the right managers to generate the necessary commitment. Or even better, by those same employees either being forced, or choosing voluntarily, to abandon the stultifying environment of the large company to set up on their own or to work for a small and young company hungry for success.

When it comes to employee motivation, big is very ugly indeed.

∾

CHAPTER 8

THE END OF THE CORPORATE MONOLITH?

'New opinions often appear first as jokes and fancies, then as blasphemies and treason, then as questions open to discussion, and finally as established truths.'

George Bernard Shaw

T he conspiracy of silence surrounding the existence of the Living Dead has involved several specific participants – Great Leaders, Esteemed Gurus, Middle Managers, the Living Dead themselves and commentators from both right and left. But the truth is that nobody has really *needed* to confront the grim truth. Indeed, it could be argued that we are all guilty, that society as a whole has been willingly complicit in this denial. The reality of incompetent, abysmally managed large corporations in which millions have wasted their lives doing very little has actually been perfectly acceptable to everyone. After all, these companies usually made nice profits, providing extremely comfortable lifestyles to those who played the corporate game astutely enough to get to the top, and a very liveable wage to those at the bottom.

In the aftermath of two murderous world wars and a devastating depression, society coveted this cosy stability. Many Western governments did their bit by offering the protection of a far-reaching welfare state. The private sector in turn had the kindness to furnish us with a warm environment where we could gradually recuperate from the stresses of the last decades. Large offices have been the spa towns of the post-war era. Compared with the Somme, Milton Keynes was a nice place to be.

The comfortable profits made by these corporations financed the welfare state. They also allowed companies to give employees the relaxed security they craved while still keeping shareholders happy. Capitalism was thus able to undergo a much-needed period of calm and consolidation, and avert the disgruntlement and social volatility which had given rise to Nazism and Soviet Communism, and which were still very much part of our collective memory. Aside from periodic race riots and violent labour disputes (both of which seem to be declining in both frequency and severity), Western societies have for the most part enjoyed decades of tranquillity and prosperity and managed to keep their populations contented. This period has therefore served its purpose. It is now drawing to a close, ushering in a new dawn of vitality, flexibility and creative individualism.

Every passing generation has the arrogance to think that its ways will struggle to be surpassed, that recent huge strides mean that we are reaching the end of the line, that progress cannot but slow down. That is, of course, until the next generation puts past ideas and structures into historical perspective. And an economy dominated by large corporations with massive payroll structures will seem in time to have been what it is – a primitive and grossly inefficient early stage of capitalism which dissipated its most valuable resource, people. As the political commentator Robin Shepherd puts it:

> 'Most of us are prone to lose historical perspective. The reality is that even in the world's most developed economies, capitalism is still very much in its infancy. Feudalism, aristocracy and clan-based rule only started to give way to capitalism in most parts of the world in the last century or two after such societies had existed themselves for thousands of years ... The idea of making workers in most industries clock on at certain times or even attend the office at all – in most cases a paternalistic ploy designed to assert authority – will start to look outmoded. Employees will increasingly have their own premises – their homes. They will negotiate their own wages, their fees, directly. They will increasingly stop becoming employees at all and start to become small businessmen. There will be profound implications for the societies in which we live.'

Our Great Leaders of the present will in time be the Great Dinosaurs of the past. Many of the more lowly will eventually cease to experience the warm glow of knowing that they will receive a regular and predictable income in return for the arduous task of ensuring that they are situated in the same place for five days a week. Instead of being paid to be physically present *in case* some work is handed to them, they will be on the outside of a greatly slimmed down corporate sector, forced to compete to sell discreet chunks of work for an agreed fee.

In order to survive and prosper, the independent worker will be motivated to ensure that his *or her* (for women will benefit particularly from the new world of work) skills and knowledge are perpetually honed to attract the necessary customers. In a marketplace that rewards innovation and hard work rather than conformity and sycophancy, he or she will be impelled to identify commercial opportunities and to anticipate future trends. Stress, the much overused and misunderstood buzzword of recent years, will no longer be the detrimental consequence of demeaning subservience and jockeying for position in the corporate rat race. It will instead become a force for good, pressuring people to contribute or face the inevitable consequences. The potential of millions will be liberated. Progress, the speed of which we have never previously encountered, will be the inevitable outcome.

A confluence of several factors is conspiring to build this world of the future, each of them reinforcing the other. Firstly, the uncovering and then open discussion of widespread structural inefficiency in the corporate world, the scale of which has never previously been acknowledged, followed by its gradual elimination by the processes of outsourcing and competition. Secondly, the individual impatience with dull lives spent in offices and the contemporary quest for meaning, as already discussed earlier in the book. Thirdly, the increased need and desire for flexibility of work. And finally, technological advance.

A gift from the grave

The Living Dead might feel that their working lives are purposeless and worthless, but they can at least console themselves that they will, indirectly, play a major role in the reshaping of our economy and the withering away of the ponderous large organization. In doing so, they will bequeath a more valuable gift to posterity than the vast majority of our Great Leaders and Esteemed Gurus put together, no matter what Warren Bennis would have us believe.

In his book *The Future of Work* written in 1984, the management author Charles Handy set out his hypothesis that jobs for life in a single company are becoming a thing of the past and that knowledge workers will in future be able to design a 'portfolio' of jobs for themselves to suit the way they wish to spend their time. Their lives will in this way become less secure but more fulfilling.

Handy's later works, *The Age of Unreason* (1990), *The Empty Raincoat* (1994) and *The Elephant and the Flea* (2001) expand on this theme and summon up a vision of the corporate future, the 'shamrock organization', consisting of three groups of people. First, there would be a small and ever-dwindling core of essential employees who would remain on permanent, full-time contracts to develop the organization and symbolize its continu- ity. The second leaf of the shamrock would represent work contracted out (or outsourced). The contractors would have a formal arrangement with the company to fulfil certain ongoing goals and responsibilities but would not work in the company as such. Lastly, there would be a flexible work force that would be employed by the company if and when required.

Those positioned on the second and third leaves of the shamrock would be free to develop their 'portfolio' lives, which might consist of salaried work, fee work, domestic work, voluntary charity work and study work. Handy writes of a different world in which large organizations are firstly trimmed down to leave only its essential centre and are then required to assume a radically altered role: 'Before very long, having a proper job inside an organization will be a minority occupation. What was a way of life for most of us will have disappeared. Organizations will still be criti- cally important in the world, but as organizers, not employers.' A host of other books, such as *Britain in 2010* by Richard Scase, published in 2000, followed Handy in forecasting a similar move away from long-term employment towards self-employment and job flexibility.

In late 2004 and early 2005, Handy's past predictions for the future of work came in for heavy criticism from the management writer Stephen Overell in an open letter in *Personnel Today*, and then in an article in the magazine *Prospect*. Overell claimed that the collapse of the career job, which Handy had foreseen, and which many others had feared, had not in fact transpired: 'Most critically, the permanent full-time job is more than ever the bedrock of work. Full-time employee posts reached a new record in November 2002 ... Well over 80% of the entire workforce is in a permanent job, full time or part time.' He might also have referred to the government statistic, quoted in the previous chapter, that a larger percent- age of the employed had been in their jobs for more than ten years in 2000 than had been in 1986 (although this particular statistic might well be a result of the large-scale structural employment of the early 1980s).

In words addressed directly to Handy, Overell writes: 'The messages you put out about work assumed the status of an orthodoxy, as manag- ers intoned: "There are no jobs for life anymore" ... This ghastly phrase became a means for employers to crack the whip, subdue dissent and justify mass redundancies ... I am not saying for a minute that you are responsible for the actions of others, any more than Christ is to blame for the crusades, or Marx for the Gulags. But I am saying that, so far, your predictions are looking shaky, and that in retrospect, you seem to have spooked us unnecessarily with dangerous phantoms that never materialized.'

This is all rather confusing. Firstly, Overell says that permanent, full-time jobs are in vogue, despite what Handy had predicted. Then he blames Handy for providing the intellectual platform for heartless corporate hatchet men to go around driving people out of permanent full-time jobs with the missionary zeal of Stalin's secret police.

So what is the true picture of the world of work today? Is it the picture painted by Overell the myth-slayer, or is it that painted by his alter ego, the Overell who believes that Handy supplied a convenient pretext for the dastardly realization of the exact same myth?

The answer provided by the statistics is mixed, as Overell himself admits. He asserts that full-time, permanent employment in Britain is buoyant and that temporary workers, who accounted for 7.2% of employees a decade ago, amount to just 6% today. On the other hand, he states that the percentage of self-employed is greater than it was twenty years ago, and that this constituency has increased quite rapidly since 2001, especially in professional occupations.

Handy, meanwhile, in a letter of reply to Overell in *Prospect*, refuted 'the comforting picture of long-term careers in old-style vertical organizations': 'About 70% of business enterprises have no employees other than the proprietor(s) while another 29% have less than 50. That doesn't leave much room for the big boys. In fact, in 2003, there were 3,415 organizations with more than 500 employees, the sort of enterprises that could and should offer long-term jobs and proper careers, but they accounted for only 9 million people.' That is, as Handy points out, 9 million out of 18 million full-time employed, 30 million who are 'economically active' and 47 million of working age. Hardly an overwhelming proportion, although it does not seem possible to discover from the available UK statistics whether it is actually decreasing.

To add what seems a further dent to the perceived credibility of Handy's predictions, these statistics *are* readily available in the United States, and the proportion of that country's workforce, full-time or part-time, in companies with more than 500 employees has increased steadily from 45.45% in 1988 to 50.13% in 2001. (Again this statistic does require qualification. As discussed in Chapter 3, large companies have tended recently to expand only through mergers and acquisitions rather than through the creation of new jobs, which according to various studies, is left in the main to smaller companies.)

The very fact that the debate between Handy and Overell is taking place shows that statistics can be used to support both their arguments, but that no clear and indisputable trend towards increased job flexibility, self-employment or smaller sized companies has yet emerged. Nevertheless, Overell is surely being premature in writing an open letter provocatively entitled, 'Dear Charles, you were wrong.' As Shepherd points out, cultural and economic trends move slowly, almost imperceptibly, but that does not mean that they are not happening. If a clear trend concerning the world of work had already emerged, Handy would not be such a stimulating and widely-read author. He is predicting for the future, based on his own personal view of what is happening now.

The existence of the Living Dead leads us to two conclusions relating to this debate. Firstly, that Handy is right in saying that the large organization will inevitably contract in size. Secondly, that this process will probably not be as quick as Handy might have once thought. No organization that allows so many workers to get paid for doing nothing for years on end can be called fast-moving or responsive.

The extreme structural inefficiency of these companies is in no way a Handy theme. In *The Empty Raincoat*, for instance, he wrote: 'Organizations are responding to the challenge of efficiency by exporting unproductive work, and people, as fast as they can. Instead of keeping a pool of slightly (*sic*) surplus labour and skills inside the organization as a sort of cushion for emergencies and comfort, they are pushing those skills outside and pulling them in when necessary.' Handy vastly underestimates the prevalence of the Living Dead and, on the flip side of the same coin, overestimates the ability of these organizations to act quickly to reduce their number.

Indeed, his view that large companies will shrink in size is not based on a negative opinion of the way they operate, but reflects his perception of an ever more sophisticated and complex world in which central corporate control is becoming 'too expensive and too complicated'. This is no doubt also the widespread view of company decision-makers. Firms have sought to outsource not because they have recognized that poor management and the sheer size of their organizations have bred apathy and inactivity, but because of the perceived lower costs of this outsourcing.

Handy also asserts that the permanent jobs which remain in these large companies are pushing people extremely hard, leading some workers to opt out of this exacting system, and thus further accelerating the process of large company contraction: 'These jobs are not for everyone. They are not for those who want more space in their lives for other things … 70 hour weeks do wear people out. At some stage, energy must yield to wisdom, or sometimes just to exhaustion. "Burn-out" would not have become such a popular jargon word if there was nothing for it to describe. We seem, in many of these very full jobs, to be cramming the 100,000 hours of a traditional lifetime's work into 30 years instead of the traditional 47 years, as in days gone by.'

✌

This book, the formal unveiling of the Living Dead, will hopefully play a role in starting to combat this still-prevailing orthodoxy about the world of work, and in making people face up to what is *really* happening. Slowly but surely, through the increasing openness and honesty of modern-day society, the scale of the Living Dead problem will become apparent. This will inevitably impact significantly on the way large companies operate, expediting the process of outsourcing that is already taking place. But even after the realization dawns, change will not be completed overnight.

It is not just the lack of responsiveness on the part of large companies that will delay progress. We also have to remember that there are an awful lot of vested interests at stake. Large numbers of people have very well-paid and cushy jobs in these companies. All those wily Professional Operators, who devote all their working days and apply all their intelligence to sustaining an image of usefulness and to developing and maintaining close alliances with those who hire and fire, are not going to be removed with ease. Companies are still often run more for the benefit of their employees than for their shareholders, a reality clearly and repeatedly demonstrated by their evident, habitual behaviour. (Just one example of many: Among the first outlays to be cut back in leaner times are training and business trips. This is recognition of the fact that they are regarded as dispensable business practices, and are offered for the most part as perks in boom times to allow staff to have a nice time out of the office at company (and thus shareholder) expense.)

Large organizations will also no doubt experience lengthy teething problems when they attempt to outsource some of their functions. A 2005 survey by the consulting firm Bain & Co found that 82% of large firms in Europe, Asia and North America are today using outsourcing firms, and 51% are outsourcing offshore. But nearly half of them said that their outsourcing programmes don't meet expectations, even when measured purely on cost improvements. Only 6% say they are 'extremely satisfied' with their outsourcing arrangements. One of the authors of the report, Mark Gottfredson, concluded that 'companies are outsourcing more and more and enjoying it less and less'.

Indeed, there has already been a backlash against the initial rush by many companies, particularly in the financial services sector, to 'offshore' some of their operations. 'Offshoring' is the process of moving jobs to another country to reduce costs by employing workers in a low-wage economy. These jobs may or may not be outsourced (i.e. companies might employ the foreign workers themselves, or they may retain the services of a foreign company).

The first area that many organizations have sought to offshore has been the customer contact centre. This has been far from popular with many customers who dislike discussing complex queries with distant-sounding, and often barely comprehensible, foreign operators. Some companies which 'offshore' have also been criticized for abandoning the domestic workforce just to save money, despite already making substantial profits. A compromise solution has now been sought in the form of 'rightshoring', a jargon word denoting the restructuring of a company's workforce to find the optimum mix of jobs performed locally and jobs moved overseas.

It will inevitably be a while before companies reach the happy equilibrium in their outsourcing strategy, which will ensure that costs are reduced and customers are satisfied. Part of this process will of course involve the intensification of competition among the companies they outsource to, the 'outsourcees', and consequently, a vast improvement in the standard of service offered by them. Let us remember that many of the specialist 'outsourcee' companies have sprung up in response to a very recent demand, and are still only a few years old. Not only will their service improve, but the relationship between them and the outsourcer will become smoother, as both sides learn from their initial mistakes and discover the most effective way to interact with each other.

During the early stages of the process, some large companies will see their relationships with independent contractors and small outsourcee companies as opportunities to wield their power and cut costs by paying low and slow. I remember working at one of my companies when there was a computer glitch that delayed the payment of monthly salary cheques by one day. The staff became distinctly restless and senior management couldn't apologize enough. Nobody might have done any work in the company in the previous month, but one day late with the money and all hell broke loose. Hard-working contractors are not afforded the same concern. As the corporate sector becomes smaller, competition to find quality outside workers will force companies to treat them better, thus removing one further psychological obstacle for workers thinking of going it alone.

Where there is revolution, there is always reaction. Those who run large companies will have to contend with the loss of control that outsourcing entails, just as they will have to learn to live with the decentralization of their own company, which will be necessary to bolster the motivation levels of their moribund staff (see previous chapter). There will undoubtedly be resistance to this dispersal of power from the centre, emanating not just from the loss of personal fiefdoms, but also from often justifiable anxieties about the efficiency of what may initially seem a more anarchic system. There will be moves by some organizations to return to the monolithic structures of the past, but those who do will be defeated by other companies, which manage to make their changes work and become more nimble and alert, with a workforce motivated to produce rather than to show up.

This will constitute the end of phase one of this period of change. But it will not just stop there for eternity so everyone can live happily ever after. Progress will continue. The outsourcees will themselves outsource, as work is performed by increasingly smaller, more specialized and more efficient units. The proportion of self-employed will grow and keep growing. The

Living Dead will seem a quaint product of a distant era. We will be interviewed on television documentaries of the future and will recount our stories to audiences watching with wide eyes and gaping mouths.

Ready, steady, go

A major theme of this book has been the incongruity between large office life and the hopes and aspirations of younger generations. It is perhaps worth briefly revisiting this topic in the context of the broader debate about the future of large organizations and the world of work.

The language ('spooking', 'dangerous phantoms') which Overell uses suggests that the fulfilment of Handy's prophecy is something to be feared. As someone who has spent years bored to tears (sometimes literally) in a large office, I think Handy's world of the future seems absolutely marvellous. All the data from earlier in the book suggest that I am not alone.

These frustrations with office life and this open intolerance of boredom will only become greater as we move even further away from the turbulent years of the first half of the twentieth century. Individual expectations will go on rising. These expectations will focus less on basic financial well-being (increasingly a given for most in wealthier societies), and more on fulfilment and meaning. For many, this fulfilment will come from making it on their own in business, thus making our economy more dynamic and productive.

Handy worries in *The Empty Raincoat* that many who will be cast off by large companies will be 'usually the people least capable of creating new work for themselves, because they lack the kind of intelligence and inclinations which would allow them to be independent. Conditioned to life as employees, we now expect them to be entrepreneurs'. A fair point (although whether large companies are discriminating and meritocratic enough to utilize the able and enterprising and discard the unintelligent is another matter, discussed at length elsewhere in this book); and of course a more independent and less secure life will not suit everybody. In the last few years, call centres have done a good job of soaking up demand for employment and maybe similar new types of job will crop up in the future for those who want them.

But to stress the point again, this impatience with office life is only just beginning to gain pace. The most eager to move voluntarily to a more independent lifestyle will initially be the talented, as they will be the most confident that they can make it in the big wide world, unprotected by a cosy career. Fashion tends to filter down rather than up. The sight of so many impressive people abandoning conventional jobs and achieving success will gradually make others aspire to the same type of working life. The percentage of people in the UK who believe that 'starting a business is a respected occupation' will rise substantially from the 38% quoted earlier in this book.

Will all the new entrepreneurs and small businesses make it, will everybody find the lifestyle they want? Of course not. Life will become tougher for many, as expectations rise and competition heats up, and there will be plenty who lack the ability or luck to make new ventures work. But tougher doesn't mean worse. Individuals seem increasingly ready to challenge themselves for a start. And it is surely better for society as a whole if more people are at least trying to contribute, rather than sitting on their backsides waiting for their next pay cheque.

Honey, we forgot the kids

Competition and the unearthing of the Living Dead will be 'push' factors in the formation of the new world of work. The quest for meaning and fulfilment is one 'pull' factor. Another will be the burgeoning demand for more flexible working lives. This is something, as we shall see, which governments should seek to encourage.

The percentage of women in the workforce has risen significantly in the last few decades. In the United States in 1998, 59.8% of women participated in the workforce, compared with 33.9% in 1950. There were a record 12.5 million women in employment in the UK in 2000, out of a total workforce of around 30 million. This figure had risen by 843,000 since 1990, with the number of men only 33,000 higher.

An increasing number of women had decided that they were no longer content with staying at home to look after the children. They had seen men acquiring money, status or fulfilment from their work and, as it became more socially acceptable for them to step outside the domestic arena, they wanted the same. Others were motivated by financial necessity or the desire to support a more expensive lifestyle.

We are perhaps now just starting to see a reaction against this trend among mothers with young families. With women entering the workplace in vast numbers, their children mostly had to be looked after by non-family members. It is never easy for parents to hand over their children to strangers, and more working women are starting to question whether, after all that, they genuinely do want to do this.

The fashion of the 1980s was money and material goods. The accent now is on fulfilment, and what could be more fulfilling than being with your children as they grow up? This change in attitude is reflected in the statistics. In a 1988 poll commissioned by *Parenting* magazine in the United States, 73% said that they would prefer to keep working full-time instead of staying at home as homemakers. This can be contrasted with a 2001 poll by Gallup/CNN/USA Today, in which only 13% of respondents said that the ideal situation was for both parents to work full-time. 41% believed that the ideal would be for one parent to work full-time while the other worked either part-time or at home and another 41% felt that one parent should stay at home solely to raise the children while the other parent works. We might also now just be starting to see this shift in mentality affecting the workplace. According to the US Census Bureau, 55% of women with newly-born babies were in the workforce in 2000 and 2002, compared with 59% in 1998, constituting the first drop in this percentage in 25 years.

More women (and men) now seem to want to combine working life with taking more responsibility for childcare, or just opt out of paid work altogether to focus on the children. How can society exact much-needed economic contribution from all these people while still satisfying their desire to care for their children? Some will have to work because of financial necessity, no matter what their preference is, but some will get by with their partner's income. Will the economy just lose them?

This is not just a problem for employers. It will also concern European governments who already know that they have to deal with a mounting demographic crisis over the next few decades. Their populations are ageing rapidly. People are living longer and producing fewer children.

In most of the 15 European Union countries before the recent expansion, fertility was lower than 1.3 children per woman (2.1 is the average required to sustain existing population levels). The UN forecasts that by 2040 in Europe as a whole, the ratio of people over 65 to those under 65 will double, from 30% to 60%. By 2050, the median age in Europe is projected to be 47.7. In some countries, such as the UK, the Netherlands and Denmark, the resulting decline in the working population will be fairly gradual. But in some, it will be extreme. In Germany, the working age population will shrink from over 51 million in 2000 to 32.8 million in 2050. The Italians are in the worst shape. Their working population will go down from 36 million to 20.9 million over this fifty-year period.

Supporting the ageing populations with state pensions and healthcare will be increasingly onerous. EU governments are already devoting more than 9% of their GDP to funding state pensions alone, and the Centre for Strategic and International Studies in Washington DC believes this could rise to 19% by 2050. As this much increased funding will have to come from a much smaller pool of people of working age (unless countries allow significant increases in immigration, which is unlikely given this policy's vote-losing potential), governments will be eager for those who are able to work to do so, even if they do have children. Action to defuse the demographic time-bomb of the future will also mean making having children as appealing as possible to those who may, for career or financial reasons, be reluctant to have them.

In many cases, governments are reacting to this challenge by throwing money at the problem, introducing one or a combination of various policies, such as child benefit packages, public childcare provision and lengthier maternity and even paternity leave after the birth of the child. Experts are divided on the success of these policies, although it is true that some countries with more generous family policies have tended to have slightly higher fertility rates. This is particularly true of France, where family support policies have helped to lift the birth rate by up to 0.5 births per woman.

But the problem with these state-sponsored strategies is that they rob Peter to pay Paul. They respond to the conundrum of funding much greater state commitments with a much smaller workforce by adding substantially to those commitments. They might enable companies to extract more contribution from mothers with small children, but it is these very same companies that will bear much of the cost of funding childcare provision through taxation.

The Labour government in the UK is planning to increase statutory maternity pay and the length of maternity leave over the next few years. Patricia Hewitt, the former Trade and Industry Secretary, stressed that this would be paid for by the taxpayer, not employers. Setting aside the fact that they *are* taxpayers, companies will also incur indirect costs, and this will impact particularly on small businesses where the temporary loss of any one employee is more keenly felt. As David Frost, Director General of the British Chambers of Commerce, said in the wake of this policy announcement: 'While the majority of any salary costs may be covered by the government's statutory pay, recruitment costs, advertising costs, retraining costs and the strain on the company will not be.' One cannot help feeling that the inevitable reaction of many small businesses to more maternity leave will be a discreet avoidance of employing younger women in the first place.

Rather than pursue these counterproductive policies, governments would be better advised to understand and then encourage incipient developments in society and the economy. A more independent working life is more compatible with child rearing, which is surely one factor explaining the disproportionate growth of female entrepreneurship (see Chapter 4).

Working from home and/or being self-employed hands time-keeping responsibility to the worker concerned. Rather than wasting hours travelling back and forth to a place of work where attendance is expected between certain immovable times of day, the independent worker can arrange work around childcare and the work demands of any partner. For the home worker, non-parental childcare will become more convenient, now being located nearby to their home *and* to their place of work. If both parents can inject this flexibility into their working lives, so much the better. More independent working lives will not only reduce the burden on the state, it will also add to the state's coffers because more people will be actually working productively rather than sitting in large offices rekindling old flames on Friends Reunited.

The independent and flexible working life will not just suit parents with young children. As governments seek to redress the balance between retirees and the working population, there will be moves to increase the age at which people receive their state pension. Moreover, the state pension itself might well have to be reduced in value, thus further encouraging pensioners to supplement their income with paid work. The workforce will therefore gradually become older. These older people might be willing and able workers, but we can assume that, for many, their willingness to work will not extend to playing corporate politics and sitting bored in interminable meetings, sandwiched in between sitting on a train for an hour and a half at either end of the day. By that age, it will be blindingly apparent, if it wasn't already, that life is too short for all that nonsense.

Smaller world, smaller office

There has been widespread misapprehension about the potential impact of modern communication technology on the world of work. With the advent of fax machines, and then e-mail and Internet, and mobile phones, and now VoIP (offering extremely cheap international telephone calls over the Internet), experts have queued up to say that all this would revolutionize the workplace. They were wrong. Other developments will revolutionize the workplace. Technology will simply facilitate the revolution.

This explains why large sections of the workforce are not already working from home, despite the existence of the technology that makes it possible. Social trends, such as the rejection of conventional large office life and the desire for flexibility of work, are still embryonic. And any corporate move towards home working, and outsourcing to small companies and independent contractors, will always take time, due to slow-moving company management, reactionary vested interests and the inevitable practical difficulties at the beginning of any process. Besides, companies are blissfully unaware of the urgent need for change. The plague of Living Death remains undiagnosed.

As all the 'push' and 'pull' factors for change coalesce, there will be much more than enough technology to allow it all to happen.

A world without Living Death

In the future, when large offices will be viewed by curious social historians as relics of a bygone age, the world will look very different.

It will be less secure and predictable, and more energetic and productive. Ever-smaller working units will be the cornerstone of the economy. Individuals will learn to stand on their own two feet. They will need to identify the skills and knowledge they need to progress and then obtain the relevant education, for themselves. They will need to find the necessary workspace and the equipment for work, for themselves. As they will not be able to rely on workplaces for social interaction and friendships, they will have to find them elsewhere, for themselves. Those who yearn for the regimented and cosseted routine of childhood to continue throughout their lives will be sadly disappointed. This will be a world for grown-ups, for people who thrive on personal responsibility.

When will this brave new world take shape? The process towards it has already begun. Unearthing the Living Dead will hasten its arrival. It's time for the denial to stop, and for the debate to begin.

☙

EPILOGUE

THE KISS OF LIFE

'Do not fear death so much as the inadequate life'.

Bertolt Brecht

I was intending to avoid addressing any words of advice directly to the Living Dead. If it were not already obvious by now, I dislike self-help books. I generally find them excessively simplistic, patronizing (hey, listen to me, yes the smug bastard over here who doesn't know you from Adam, I'll tell you how to run your life better), and have always found them totally useless. I was going to concentrate purely on an overview of current trends in the modern workplace and on how companies could improve the way they operate.

But then in February 2005 I wrote a short article in *The Times* on the subject of this book, the unspoken truth of millions of people being left to rot, bored out of their minds in large organizations. How could it be, I wrote, that we have accepted unquestioningly the ubiquitous received wisdom that everyone nowadays is overworked, when the statistics, which are staring us right in the face, are suggesting a very different story?

Predictably, but nevertheless interestingly, the e-mails I received in response to the article from those people still employed in the organization about which they were writing, were anonymous (i.e. they wrote from private e-mail addresses that did not give away their full name). I can imagine that they were still nervous about doing even that, but they had an overwhelming urge to convey their agreement with the substance of my article. Plenty more, I suspect, refrained from writing because they did not have an e-mail address that maintained their anonymity. Here, in a nutshell, is the main obstacle we face in improving the quality of our working lives and therefore the productivity of our economy. To progress, we need an open discussion of the problem, and that is so difficult to achieve when people understandably fear for their livelihoods for speaking the truth.

Most of the content of the e-mails centred around experiences which backed up what I had written. One woman wrote: 'I completely agree with everything – middle managers cannot see the boredom below them and I have therefore decided that I cannot sit bored stiff any longer. I have disguised course notes and I study in the office, shuffling paper with vigour, carrying my notes to the toilet, and sighing gently at the workload … I pay my credit card bills, study and sort out my bank statements, catch up with friends in a foreign language, occasionally dropping our company name into the conversation along with Anglicized words such as sales, meeting, products, for fun.'

Another e-mail was from a man who had recently set up his own business after becoming disillusioned with his corporate career, where he had been employed in roles that conjure up an instant image of dynamic lifestyles, challenging work and late nights (he had acted as a lawyer, private client adviser in a Big 4 accountancy firm and a private banker in the City). The picture he paints though is rather different: 'I came across plenty of bored people, effectively shuffling paper/trying to justify an existence in their employment – these were divided between those who wanted to do more/be useful but weren't given the opportunity, and those who knew they were getting paid (sometimes very well paid) to do very little but were happy just to take the money, sometimes the power and the glory, and keep quiet about it!' More or less the perfect definition of the Living Dead and the Professional Operators.

But it was an e-mail exchange with another man that persuaded me to write this short epilogue. He clearly was at the end of his tether: 'I've got a career book and am trying to work out what direction to go in to avoid falling into a job that doesn't have much work to do. If you don't mind me asking, how did you make the leap from insurance to journalism? I keep looking at office jobs as that's the only experience I have, but I suppose that'll leave me in the same place as I am now. And do you have any advice as to how I'll know whether the department I'm looking round is busy, or being 'talked up' – twice in my internal transfers I've been told that the unit is busy, to the extent where they're taking on numerous staff not just me, to find out it was all talk and there's not enough to do. How can I avoid this in the future?'

How many thousands or millions of others, I wondered, were in an identical position. Bored for years in their jobs, but nevertheless still retaining that deep-seated urge to contribute something worthwhile, to utilize the abilities they were born with. If there were people who really did want advice from me about how to escape their Living Death, what would I tell them?

The first thing I would suggest is to seek out small operations. That is not to say that there are no hard-working people in large companies. Of course there are. But the larger the company, the less transparent the activities of the workers tend to be. Consequently, politics rather than productive work becomes the way to get ahead. This would not be an appropriate environment for those who crave real achievement rather than superficial status. If you do want to stay in a large company, seek out the small and tightly-knit working units that have clearly defined and measurable goals and an obviously useful purpose.

Not only will a small unit be more conducive to real work, you are likely to feel more valued. In a company of five, one excellent member of staff verges on the indispensable. This could not be said of anyone in a company of fifty thousand. You are therefore less likely to enter the downward spiral which consigns so many to an early Living Death: Nobody seems to notice around here whether I am doing a good job or not → I'll take it easy for a while, I'm feeling tired at the moment, new-born at home wearing me out → It really is true. Nobody did notice that I accomplished the square root of f**k all for the last three months → Would anyone blink an eye if I defenestrated myself? → OK, right, let's analyze this calmly. I'm getting paid to show up. There's nothing to be gained by working. There's nothing to be lost by not working. On the occasions when I do have work to do, I find it quite boring. Hmm, what should I … Oh no, look what Brian's sent me. Oh please … a camel and a zebra at it like there's no tomorrow! He's one sick bastard.'

Finding the right manager to work for is crucial. The vast majority are terrible, habitually allowing able and energetic people to slump into a slough of despond, so this will not be easy. You will need all your wits about you to work out before you take the job whether the person in question has the ability to motivate and inspire you over the long-term. Do you think he is genuinely interested in you, in finding out what makes you tick and getting the best out of you? Is he focused on managing, rather on his own personal agenda? If he utters the lazy manager trick of saying, 'This is a company where you create your own opportunities,' or 'Here, we show commitment to people when they've shown commitment to us,' walk straight out, stopping only to turn your nose up and utter those key words, 'That great management guru Bolchover would think you were an idiot.'

Sniff out signs of life and openness in the company or department you are looking at. Again, never easy, for as my e-mail correspondent said, people are often better at talking themselves up than at doing any work. Evidence of people regularly changing roles indicates a fluid energy and an emphasis on motivating people and keeping them interested. A policy of frequent home working reveals a culture which values product over posturing. Too much jargon and too many people talking in riddles are sure signs that image is paramount and meritocracy is absent. In this atmosphere, performance and hard work are relegated a long way down the league table of priorities.

Does the company concerned operate in a genuinely competitive environment? If it does, the talents of each individual will need to be stretched to the full. If we are talking about a huge company in an industry dominated by a small number of huge companies, any naïve dreams of being pushed or stretched stand to be well and truly crushed. The absence of competition in the public sector is likely to result in a similarly dispiriting scenario there.

One sure way to expose yourself to competition is to set up a company, either on your own or with others. You might fail, you might worry yourself into an early grave, but it is unlikely that you will be bored. Not everyone is cut out for this (although an increasing number will be), but the best of luck if you try. Enterprise is the lifeblood of our economy. CEO of massive operation – sorry, doesn't impress me. Go and do something useful. Bloke down the road working all hours on his own to support his family and to bring his business idea to fruition. Hero.

Always try to seek the type of work that gives you large amounts of energy, so that you may still have some in reserve when the working environment and/or your manager are both trying their damnedest to deplete it. As the Gallup consultant and author Marcus Buckingham said: 'Find out what you don't like doing and stop doing it. Your greatest opportunity comes from your strengths – too many people think it's about working on their weaknesses.' Too right, and if your manager harps on about your weaknesses the whole time, rather than trying to find your strengths and then harness them to the needs of the business, it may be time for you to bid farewell, and for him to go off and do something he's good at.

The legendary late American chat show host, Johnny Carson, once said: 'Never continue in a job you don't enjoy. If you're happy in what you're doing, you'll like yourself, you'll have inner peace. And if you have that, along with physical health, you will have had more success than you could possibly have imagined.' Easy to say perhaps for someone who for thirty years spent his evenings sitting talking to the likes of Groucho Marx and Woody Allen, and who no doubt had a couple of hundred mill safely tucked away in his local Woolwich. But he was right, nonetheless.

∾

INDEX

Printed in the USA/Agawam, MA
January 26, 2015

607335.018